VALUE AND VALUES
IN EVOLUTION

VALUE AND VALUES
IN EVOLUTION

Edited by

EDWARD A. MAZIARZ

Loyola University of Chicago

GORDON AND BREACH
New York   London   Paris

Gordon and Breach, Science Publishers, Inc.
One Park Avenue
New York, NY10016

Gordon and Breach Science Publishers Ltd.
42 William IV Street
London WC2N 4DF

Gordon & Breach
7-9 rue Emile Dubois
Paris 75014

Library of Congress Cataloging in Publication Data
Main entry under title:

Value and values in evolution.

   Lectures delivered at a symposium entitled "Current
evolution of man's sense of values" sponsored by Loyola
University of Chicago on the occasion of its centenary
celebration in 1970.
   Includes index.
1. Values—Congresses. I. Maziarz, Edward A.
II. Loyola University, Chicago.
BD232.V26   121'.8   78-19561
ISBN 0—677—15240—X

Acknowledgement. To The University of Chicago Press for Mircea Eliade,
"The World, the City, and the House," from *Occultism, Witchcraft, and
Cultural Fashions*, pp. 18-31 (Chapter 2).

Preface

The lectures contained in this book were delivered at a Symposium entitled "Current Evolution of Man's Sense of Values." As such, the lectures represent but one element of a large number of addresses, symposia, and convocations sponsored by Loyola University of Chicago on the occasion of its Centenary celebration.

It might assist the reader to be appraised, beforehand, of some common themes embodied in the following articles. Central to each of them is the call to urgency in resolving those issues that prevent men from having value-freedom instead of value-bondage. And thus, instead of opting for a scholarly quietism about the present condition of man, the contributors to this volume are expectant that their scholarly work will, in the expression of one of the participants, make men more creative of values by opening to them the possibility of mutually recreating men.

Secondly, the participants in this symposium presuppose that reason alone cannot resolve the issue of values. On the one hand, reason needs to be abetted and supported by the vision of hope. Unlinked to hope, reason may remain but a prisoner to empty vacuities and futile abstractions. On the other hand, reason also needs the support of a communal faith before is can issue into action that is conservative of some old and determinative of some new values.

Thirdly, the contributors to this volume presuppose that the issues of values in the human future is not the concern of one particular academic discipline, nor of one unique power structure. Their contributions emphasize the new significance and relevance that the notion of values offers to all scholarly endeavors. The search for values — formerly associated with the arts and humanities — is now recognized as permeating the social and the natural sciences as well. In addition, the rubric of value has helped to clarify the powerful agency that each human being exercises in preserving and in creating new values not only in his immediate neighborhood but also within the wider reaches of the social, political, and international orders as well.

For their advice and personal support in planning the Symposium, I am grateful to my colleagues, Francis J. Catania and Kenneth F. Thompson, and to the University Director of the Centenary, John Borgard, and his wife, Peggy. A number of friends and graduate students also assisted me in countless ways, and among them I want to mention especially Jean Trudeau, Rita Brennan, and Zelda Catania for their secretarial assistance, and Robert D. Ricketts and Justin Synnestvedt for their invaluable help in coordinating the many large and small tasks associated with the Values Symposium.

EDWARD A. MAZIARZ
Loyola University of Chicago

Contents

PART I

VALUES AND RELIGIOUS FAITH

The World, the City, and the House

Mircea Eliade

Years ago, one of my professors at the University of Bucharest had the opportunity to attend a series of lectures given by the famous historian, Theodore Mommsen. At that time in the early 1890s, Mommsen was already very old, but his mind was still lucid and harbored a memory that was astonishingly complete and accurate. In his first lecture, Mommsen was describing Athens during the time of Socrates. He went to the blackboard and traced, without a single note, the plan of the city as it was in the fifth century; and then he proceeded to indicate the temples and public buildings, as well as showing where some of the famous wells and groves were situated. Particularly impressive was his vivid reconstruction of the environmental background of the *Phaedrus*. After quoting the passage when Socrates inquires where Lysias was staying, and Phaedrus replies that he was staying with Epicrates, Mommsen pointed out the possible location of Epicrates' house, explaining that the text states that "the house where Morychus used to live" was "close to the temple of Olympian Zeus." Mommsen continued by graphically displaying the walk of Socrates and Phaedrus along the river Ilissus, during which he indicated the probable place of the memorable dialogue at "the quiet spot" where the "tall plane tree" grew.

Awed by Mommsen's amazing display of erudition, memory, and literary insight, my professor was reluctant to leave the amphitheater immediately after the lecture. He, then, noticed that an elderly valet came forward and gently took Mommsen's arm, guiding him out of the amphitheater. At this point, one of the students still present explained that

3

the famous historian did not know how to go home alone.
The greatest living authority on fifth century Athens was
completely lost in his own city of Wilhelmian Berlin!

For what I intend to discuss this morning, I could hardly
find a better introduction. Mommsen admirably illustrates
the existential meaning of "living in one's own world." His
real world, the only one which was relevant and meaningful,
was the classical, Graeco-Roman world. For Mommsen, the
world of the Greeks and Romans was not simply *history*, that
is a dead past recovered through a historiographical
anamnesis; it was *his* world — that place where he could
move, think, and enjoy the beatitude of being alive and
creative. I do not really know if he always required a servant
to guide him to his home. Probably not. Most likely, as most
creative scholars, he lived in two worlds: the Universe of
forms and values, to the understanding of which he dedicated
his life, and which corresponds somehow to the "cosmi-
cized," and therefore "sacred" world of the primitives; and
the everyday, "profane" world into which he was "thrown,"
as Heidegger would say. But then, in his old age, Mommsen
obviously felt detached from the profane, nonessential, and
for him meaningless and ultimately chaotic space of modern
Berlin. If one can speak of an amnesia with regard to the
profane space of Berlin, one has also to recognize that this
amnesia was compensated by an incredible *anamnesis* of all
that concerned Mommsen's existential world, i.e. the classical
Graeco-Roman universe. In his old age, Mommsen was living
in a world of archetypes.

Perhaps the closest parallel to this experience of feeling
lost in an unknown, chaotic space is found among the
Achilpa, one of the Australian Aranda tribes. According to
their mythology, a divine being called Numbakula "cosmi-
cized" their territory, created their ancestor, and founded
their institutions. Numbakula fashioned a sacred pole out of
the trunk of a gum tree, climbed up to the sky on it and
disappeared. This pole represents the cosmic axis, for it is
around it that the land becomes habitable and is transformed
into a "world." For this reason the ritual role of the sacred
pole is a considerable one: the Achilpa carry it with them in

their wanderings and decide which direction to take according to the way it leans. This allows them, in spite of their
continual moving about, always to find themselves in "their
world" and at the same time to remain in communication
with the heaven into which Numbakula has vanished. If the
pole is broken, it is a catastrophe; in a way, it is the "end of
the world" and a regression into chaos. Spencer and Gillen
relate a legend in which the sacred pole was broken and the
entire tribe fell prey to anguish. The people wandered hap-
hazardly for a time and finally sat down on the ground and
allowed themselves to perish.[1] † This is an excellent illustra-
tion of the necessity for "cosmicizing" the land which is to
be lived in. The "world," for the Achilpa, becomes "their
world" only to the degree in which it reproduces the cosmos
organized and sanctified by Numbakula. They cannot live
without this vertical axis which assures an "opening" toward
the transcendent and at the same time makes possible their
orientation in space. In other words, one cannot live in a
"chaos." Once this contact with the transcendent is broken
off and the system of orientation disrupted, existence in the
world is no longer possible — and so the Achilpa let themselves die.[2]

No less dramatic is the case of the Bororo of the Matto
Grosso in Brazil, which is brilliantly discussed by Claude
Levi-Strauss in his book, *Tristes Tropiques*. Traditionally, the
Bororo village was organized in a rough circle around the
men's house and the dancing ground; and it was also divided
into four quarters by two axes — one running north to south
and the other east to west. These divisions governed the
whole social life of the village, especially its system of inter-
marriage and kinship. The Salesian missionaries who first
dealt with this tribe thought that the only way to help them,
was to persuade them to leave their traditional village and
settle in a new one. The charitable and well-meaning missionaries established what they thought to be a more convenient
and practical village of rectangular huts set out in parallel
rows. This reorganisation completely destroyed the complex

---

† Numbered footnotes are collected at the end of each chapter.

Bororo social system, which was so closely bound to the
layout of the traditional village that it could not survive
transplantation into a different physical environment. What
was even more tragic was that the Bororo, in spite of their
quasi-nomadic way of life, felt completely disoriented in the
world once they were removed from their traditional cosmology depicted in the village plan. Under these conditions,
they accepted any other plausible explanation offered by the
Salesians for their new and confusing Universe.[3]

Ultimately, for the man of archaic society, the very fact
of *living in the world has a religious value.* For he lives in a
world which has been created by Supernatural Beings and
where his village or house is an image of the Cosmos. The
cosmology does not yet possess profane, protoscientific
values and functions. The cosmology, that is the cosmological images and symbols which inform the habitable world,
is not only a system of religious ideas, but also a pattern of
religious behavior.

But if living in the world for archaic man has a religious
value, this is a result of a specific experience of what can be
called "sacred space." Indeed, for religious man, space is not
homogeneous; some parts of space are qualitatively different.
There is a sacred space, and hence a strong, significant space;
and there are other spaces that are not sacred and so are
without structure, form, or meaning. Nor is this all. For
religious man, this spatial nonhomogeneity finds expression
in the experience of an opposition between space that is
sacred — the only *real* and *really* existing space — and all
other spaces, the formless expanse surrounding it. The religious experience of the nonhomogeneity of space is a primordial experience, comparable to the founding of the world.
For it is the break effected in space that allows the world
to be constituted, because it reveals the fixed point, the
central axis for all future orientation. When the sacred mani-
fests itself in any hierophany, there is not only a break in
the homogeneity of space; there is also a revelation of an
absolute reality, opposed to the nonreality of the vast
surrounding expanse. The manifestation of the sacred onto-
logically creates the world. In the homogeneous and infinite

expanse, in which no point of reference is possible and hence no *orientation* can be established, the hierophany reveals an absolute fixed point, a *center*.

So it is clear to what a great degree the discovery — that is, the revelation — of a sacred space possesses existential value for religious man; for nothing can begin, nothing can be *done*, without a previous orientation — and any orientation implies acquiring a fixed point. It is for this reason that religious man has always sought to fix his abode at the "center" of the world." *If the world is to be lived in*, it must be *founded* — and no world can be born in the chaos of the homogeneity and relativity of profane space. The discovery or projection of a fixed point — the center — is equivalent to the creation of the world. Ritual orientation and construction of sacred space has a cosmogonic value; for the ritual by which man constructs a sacred space is efficacious in the measure in which *it reproduces the work of the gods*, i.e. the cosmogony.

The history of Rome, as well as the history of other cities or peoples, begins with the *foundation of the town*; that is to say, the *foundation* is tantamount to a *cosmogony*. Every new city represents a new beginning of the world. As we know from the legend of Romulus, the ploughing of the circular ditch. the *sulcus primigenis*, designates the foundation of the city walls. The classical writers were tempted to derive the word *urbs* ("city") from *urvums*, the curve of a ploughshare, or *urvo*, "I plough round"; some of them derived it from *orbis*, a curved thing, a globe, the world. And Servius[4] mentions "the custom of the ancients (which decreed) that as a new town was founded by the use of a plough, so it should also be destroyed by the same rite by which it was founded."

The center of Rome was a hole, *mundus*, the point of communication between the terrestrial world and the lower regions. Roscher has long since interpreted the *mundus* as an *omphalos* (i.e. navel of the earth); every town possessing a *mundus* was thought to be situated in the Center of the World, in the navel of *orbis terrarum*. It has also been rightly proposed that *Roma quadrata* is to be understood not as being square in shape, but as being divided into four parts. Roman cosmology was based on the image of *terra* divided into four regions.[5]

Similar conceptions are to be found everywhere in the neolithic and postneolithic world. In India, the town, as well as the temple, is built in the likeness of the Universe. The foundation rites represent the repetition of the cosmogony. In the center of the town there is symbolically located Mt. Meru, the cosmic mountain, together with the high gods; and also each of the four principle gates of the town are under the protection of a god. In a certain sense, the town and its inhabitants are elevated to a superhuman plane; the city is assimilated into Mt. Meru, and the inhabitants become the "images" of the gods. Even as late as the eighteenth century, Jaipur was built after the traditional model described in the *Silpa-sastra*.[6]

The Iranian metropolis had the same plan as the Indian towns, that is it was an *imago mundi*. According to the Iranian tradition, the Universe was conceived as a wheel with six spokes and a large hole in the middle, like a navel. The texts proclaim that the "Iranian country" (*Airyanem vaejah*) is the center and the heart of the world; consequently, it is the most precious among all the other countries. For that reason, Shiz, the town where Zarathustra was born, was regarded as the source of royal power. The throne of Khosru II was constructed in such a way as to symbolize the Universe. The Iranian king was called "Axis of the World," or "World's pole." Seated on the throne, in the middle of his palace, the king was symbolically situated at the center of the cosmic town, the Uranopolis.[7]

This type of cosmic symbolism is even more striking with regard to Angkor in Cambodia. "The city with its walls and moats represents the World surrounded by its chains of mountains and by the mythical oceans. The temple in the center symbolizes Mt. Meru, its five towers standing up like the five peaks of the sacred Mountain. Its subordinate shrines represent the constellations in their courses, i.e. the Cosmic Time. The principal ritual act imposed on the faithful consists in walking round the building in the prescribed

direction, so as to pass in succession through each stage of
the solar cycle, in other words to traverse space in step with
time. The temple is in fact a chronogram, symbolizing and
controlling the sacred cosmography and topography of the
Universe, of which it is the ideal center and regulator."[8]

With some variations, we find the same pattern everywhere
in South-East Asia. Siam was divided into four provinces,
with the metropolis in the middle; and in the center of the
town stood the royal palace. The country was thus an image
of the Universe, for according to the Siamese cosmology, the
Universe is a quadrangle with Mt. Meru in the middle. Bang-
kok is called the "the celestial royal city," "the city of the
Gods," etc. The king, placed in the center of the world, was
a *cakravartin*, a Cosmocrator. Likewise, in Burma, Mandalay
was built, in 1857, according to the traditional cosmology;
that is as an *imago mundi* — quadrangular and having the
royal palace in the center. We find in China the same cosmological pattern, and the same correlation between cosmos-
state-city-palace. The world was conceived as a rectangle
having China in the middle; on the four horizons were
situated four seas, four holy mountains, and the four bar-
barian nations. The town was built as a quadrangle, with
three gates on each side, and with the palace at the center,
corresponding to the Polar Star. From this center, the perfect
sovereign was able to influence the whole Universe.[9]

It is a mistake to think that this cosmological symbolism
was restricted to palaces, temples, and royal capitals, and that
such symbols were intelligible only to the learned theologians
and the rich and powerful sovereigns, administrators, and
aristocrats. For obvious reasons, I have referred to some of
the most famous examples of architectural construction; but
we also find the same cosmological symbolism in the structure of any house, hut, or tent of traditional societies, even
among the most archaic and "primitive."

As a matter of fact, it is usually not possible to speak of
the house without referring to the city, the sanctuary, or the
World. In many cases, what can be said of the house, applies
equally to the village or the town. The multiple homologies —
between cosmos, land, city, temple, palace, house, and hut

— emphasize the same fundamental symbolism: everyone of these images expresses the existential experience of *being in the World*, more exactly of being situated in an organized and meaningful world (i.e. organized and meaningful because it was created by the Supernatural Beings). The same cosmological symbolism, formulated in spatial architectonic terms, informs the house as well as the city of the universe. To understand the symbolism of a Dayak house, one must know the cosmogonic myth, namely that the world came into being as a result of a combat between two polar principles, the Supreme Deity Mahatala and the Primordial Water Snake. For every house is a replica of the primeval exemplary house, and thus it is symbolically erected on the back of the Water-snake, its roof corresponds to the primeval mountain on which Mahatala is enthroned, and an umbrella represents the Tree of Life. In the same way, the cosmological dualism characteristic of Indonesian religion, culture, and society, is clearly seen in the structure of every Indonesian house with its ritually consecrated "male" and "female" divisions.[10]

The traditional Chinese town is similarly informed by a cosmic symbolism. The opening in the roof, called "window of the Heaven," assures communication with Heaven. The Chinese applied the same term to the opening of the Mongolian tent. This term — "window of the Heaven" — also means in Chinese "chimney." The Mongolian tent is constructed with a central pole which emerges through the upper hole. This post is symbolically identified with the "Pillar of the World," i.e. with the *axis mundi*. In many parts of the world this *axis mundi* has been concretely represented either by the central pillar that supports the house, or in the form of isolated stakes called "World Pillars." In other words, *cosmic symbolism is found in the very structure of everyday habitation*. The house is an *imago mundi*. Because the sky was conceived as a vast tent supported by a central pillar, the tent pole, or the central post of the house, was assimilated to the Pillars of the World and was so named.[11]

Similar conceptions are found among many North American Indian tribes, especially the Algonquins and the Sioux. Their sacred lodge, where initiations are performed, represents the Universe. The roof symbolizes the dome of the sky, the floor represents earth, the four walls the four directions of cosmic space. The ritual construction of the sacred space is emphasized by a threefold symbolism: the four doors, the four windows, and the four colors all signify the four cardinal points. The construction of the sacred lodge thus repeats the cosmogony, for the lodge represents the world. We may also add that the interdependence between the Cosmos and Cosmic Time ("circular" time) was so strongly felt that in several Indian languages, the term for "World" is also used to mean "year." For example, certain California tribes say "the world is past," or "the earth is passed," to mean that "a year has passed." The Dakotas say: the "Year is a circle around the World," that is, a circle around the sacred cabin.[12]

Perhaps the most revealing example is the house symbolism of the Fali, a people of the North Cameroun. The house is the image of the Universe, and consequently of the microcosm represented by man; but it reflects at the same time all the phases of the cosmogonic myth. In other words, the house is not a static construction, but has a "movement" corresponding to the different stages of the cosmogonic process. The orientation of the separate units (the central pole, the walls, the roof) as well as the position of the tools and furniture, are related to the movements of the inhabitants and their location in the house. That is to say, the members of the family change their places inside the habitation in respect to the seasons, the time of the day, and the various modifications of their familial or social status.[13]

I have said enough about the religious significance of human dwelling places for certain conclusions to have become almost self-evident. Exactly like the city or the sanctuary, the house is sanctified, in whole or part, by a cosmological symbolism or ritual. This is why settling somewhere — building a village or merely a house — represents a serious decision, for the very existence of man is involved; he must, in short, create his own world and assume the responsibility of maintaining and renewing it. Habitations are not lightly changed, for it is not easy to abandon one's world.

The house is not an object, a "machine to live in"; *it is the universe that man constructs for himself by imitating the paradigmatic creation of the gods, the cosmogony.* Every construction and every inauguration of a new building are in some measure equivalent to a *new beginning*, a *new life.* And every beginning repeats the primordial beginning, when the Universe first saw the light of day. Even in modern societies, with their high degree of desacralization, the festivity and rejoicing that accompany settling in a new house still preserve the memory of the festive exuberance that, long ago, marked the *incipit vita nova.*

I do not think that we can dismiss all these beliefs and experiences on the ground that they belong to the past and have no relevance for modern man. The scientific understanding of cosmic space which has no center and is infinite has nothing to do with the existential experience of living in a familiar and meaningful world. Even such a *history*-oriented people as the Jews could not live without a cosmological framework comparable to some of the patterns which I have been discussing this morning. The Jews also believe that Israel is located at the center of the world and that the foundation Stone of the Temple in Jerusalem represents the foundation of the world. The rock of Jerusalem reached deep into the subterranean waters (*tehom*). The Temple was situated exactly above the *tehom*, the Hebrew equivalent of the Babylonian *apsu*, the primeval waters before Creation. The *apsu* and the *tehom* symbolize the aquatic chaos, the *preformal modality of cosmic matter*, and at the same time, the world of death, of all that precedes and follows life. The rock of Jerusalem designates not only the point of intersection — and hence of communication — between the lower world and earth, but also *the difference in ontological status between these two cosmic planes.* The lower regions can be related to the unknown, desert regions that surround the inhabited territory; the underworld, over which the cosmos is firmly established, corresponds to the chaos that extends to its frontiers.[14]

Consequently, Jerusalem is "that one place on earth which is closest to heaven, which is horizontally the exact center of the geographical world and vertically the exact midpoint between the upper world and the lower world, the place where both are closest to the skin of the earth, heaven being only two or eighteen miles above the earth at Jerusalem, the waters of *Tehom* lying only a thousand cubits below the temple floor. For the Jew to journey up to Jerusalem is to ascend to the very crucible of creation, the womb of everything, the center and fountain of reality, the place of blessing *par excellence*.[15]

For that reason Israel is, as Rabbi Nachman of Bratislava puts it, the "real center of the spirit of life and therefore of the renewal of the world . . ., the spring of joy, the perfection of wisdom, . . . the pure and healing power of the earth."[16] The vital power of the land and the Temple is expressed in a variety of ways, and the rabbis often appear to vie with each other in contests of exaggeration. In the same sense, a rabbinical text asserts that "when the Temple was ruined, the blessing departed from the world." As the historian of religions, Jonathan Z. Smith, interprets this rabbinical tradition: "The Temple and its ritual serve as the cosmic pillars or the 'sacred pole' supporting the world. If its service is interrupted or broken, if an error is made, then the world, the blessing, the fertility, indeed all of creation which flows from the Center, will likewise be disrupted. Like the Achilpa's sacred pole . . ., the disruption of the Center and its power is a breaking of the link between reality and the world, which is dependent upon the Sacred Land. Whether through error or exile, the severing of this relationship is a cosmic disaster."[17]

Contemporary Jewish scholars and writers as different as Chaim Raphael, David Ben Gurion, Richard L. Rubenstein, and Jonathan Smith utilize similar cosmological images when they try to express what the Exile meant for the Jews. "While the exile is an event which can be located chronologically as after A.D. 70," writes Jonathan Smith, it is above all a thoroughly mythic event: "the return to chaos, the de-creation, the separation from the deity analogous to the total catastrophe of the primeval flood."[18] The loss of Jerusalem, writes Chaim Raphael, meant more than the historical event of the Jews driven into exile: "God himself was in exile. The world was out of joint. The destruction was the symbol of it."[19] Of course, the "homeless God," the Presence of God exiled, are images previously used by Rabbi Akiba in the first century; but it is highly significant that they are so popular today. Jonathan Eibschutz, an eighteenth century Talmudist, writes: "If we do not have Jerusalem . . . why should we have life? . . . Surely we have descended from life unto death. And the converse is true. When the Lord restores the captivity of Zion we shall ascend from death unto life."[20] It is striking that "even among the so-called atheistic, secularist, deeply Marxist Zionists who founded the first *Kibutzim*, their religion of 'land and labor' is a resurgence of the old language of a recovered center, of life shared with the land. Thus, for example, A.D. Gordon, understood by many to be the leader of the secular communitarians in the early twentieth century, describes their experience in a language resplendent with overtones of cosmic trees, world navels, and so forth: 'It is life we want, writes A.D. Gordon, no more no less than that, our own life feeding on our vital sources, in the fields and under the skies of our Homeland . . . We come to our Homeland in order to be planted in our natural soil from which we have been uprooted . . . It is our duty to concentrate all our strength on this central spot . . . What we seek to establish in Palestine is a new re-created Jewish people.' "[21]

I could easily multiply quotations, and of course, I could add many comparable examples from other modern cultures. I have stressed Jewish cosmological symbolism because it is less familiar:[22] as a matter of fact, Judaism, and to a certain extent, Christianity, are generally regarded as being almost entirely *historical*, that is *time*-oriented religions. The land of Israel, with Jerusalem and the Temple in the center, is a sacred country because it has a *sacred history* consisting of the long and fabulous series of events, planned and carried out by Jahweh for the benefit of His people. But this is true for many other religions, primitive as well as Oriental. The land of the Aranda, of the Dayak, and of the Bororo is sacred because it was created and organized by Supernatural Beings: the cosmogony is only the beginning of a sacred history, which is followed by the creation of man and other mythical events.

I do not need to discuss here the similarities and differences between the so-called primitive, *cosmic* religions and the *historical*, biblical faiths. What is relevant for our theme is the fact that everywhere we find the same fundamental conception of the necessity to live in an intelligible and meaningful world, and that this conception emerges ultimately from the experience of a sacred space. Now one can ask in what sense such experiences of the sacred space of houses, cities, and lands are still significant for the modern de-sacralized man. Certainly, we know that man never lived in the space conceived by mathematicians and physicists as being isotropic, that is space having the same properties in all directions. The space experienced by man is *oriented*, and thus anisotropic, for each dimension and direction has a specific value; for instance, along the vertical axis, "up" does not have the same value as "down"; along the horizontal axis, left and right may be differentiated in value. The question is whether the experience of oriented space, and other comparable experiences of intentionally structured spaces (for example, the different spaces of art and architecture) have something in common with the sacred space known by *homo religiosus.*

This is, surely, a difficult question — but *who* can be expected to offer an answer? Certainly not someone who is unaware of what sacred space means, and who totally ignores the cosmic symbolism which I discussed this morning. Unfortunately, this is very often the case.

I would like to conclude by reminding you of that famous lawsuit which followed Brancusi's first exhibition at the Armory Show in New York. The New York customs refused to admit that some of Brancusi's sculptures — for example, *Mlle. Pogany* and *A Muse* — were really works of art, and taxed them very heavily as if they were blocks of marble. We must not be overly harsh in our judgement of the New York customs agents, for during the subsequent lawsuit over the taxation of Brancusi's works, at least one of the leading American art critics declared that *Mlle. Pogany* and *A Muse* were merely pieces of polished marble!

Brancusi's art was so *new* that, in 1913, even some art specialists could not *see* it. Likewise, the cosmic symbolism of sacred space is so *old* and so *familiar* that many are not yet able to recognize it.

Endnotes

1.   B. Soencer and F.J. Gillen: *The Arunta*. London, 1926. I, p. 388.
2.   Mircea Eliade: *The Sacred and the Profane*. New York, 1959. pp. 31-39.
3.   Claude Levi-Strauss: *Tristes tropiques*. Paris, 1955. pp. 227ff; Joseph Rykwert: *The Idea of a Town* (reprinted from *Forum*, Hilversum, n.d.). p. 41.
4.   In IV *Aen*. 212; cf. Rykwert, *op. cit.*
5.   Cf. *The Sacred and the Profane*. p. 47; see also "Centre du Monde, Temple, Maison," *Le Symbolisme Cosmique des Monuments Religious*. Roma, 1957, pp. 57-82.
6.   Cf. Stella Kramrish: *The Hindu Temple*. Calcutta, 1946. I, pp. 14ff., 26ff., etc.; and our forthcoming book *The Center of the World*.
7.   See the sources quoted in *The Center of the World*.
8.   Bernard-Philippe Groslier and Jacques Arthaud: *The Arts and Civilization of Angkor*. New York, 1957, p. 30.
9.   For the references see *The Center of the World*.
10. Cf. Mircea Eliade: *The Quest*. Chicago, 1969. pp. 77ff., 160ff.
11. See our article "Briser le Toit de la Maison," *Studies in Mysticism and Religion, Presented to Gershom Scholem*. Jerusalem, 1967. pp. 131-39; and *Center of the World*. Chapters III-IV.
12. Cf. *The Sacred and the Profane*. pp. 46, 73-74.
13. See J.-P. Lebeuf: *L'habitation des Fali montagnards du Cameroun septentrional*. Paris, 1961. pp. 457ff.
14. See the sources quoted in *The Myth of the Eternal Return*. New York, 1959. pp. 7ff.; *The Sacred and the Profane*. pp. 36ff.
15. Jonathan Z. Smith: "Earth and Gods," *The Journal of Religion*. XLIX, 1969. pp. 103-27, p. 112.
16. Quoted by J.Z. Smith: *op. cit.* p. 113.
17. Smith: *op. cit.* p. 117.
18. *Ibid.* p. 118.
19. Quoted by J.Z; Smith: *op. cit.* p. 120, n. 41.
20. Quoted *ibid.* p. 119.
21. Quoted *ibid.* pp. 125-26.
22. But see also Richard L. Rubenstein: "The Cave, the Rock, and the Tent: the Meaning of Place," *Continuum*. 1968. pp. 143-55.

Religions and Changing Values

R. Ninian Smart

The study of religion is essentially a very recent growth in the history of human enquiry. Like so many other novelties it is a product largely of the nineteenth century; but perhaps only in the latter part of the twentieth century will it come fully into its own, through the synthesis of various methodological approaches — philological, hermenutic, sociological, historical, psychological.

One of the striking perceptions of recent study of religion has been the recognition of the necessity to treat religious changes not merely in terms of religious experience, doctrine and practice narrowly considered, but also in terms of the social dimension. It is thus not possible to discuss the future evolution of religious values except by noticing certain tendencies in human institutions and societies. In this lecture I permit myself the luxury of speculating along these lines, and placing the religious situation in the political and cultural setting of the modern world. But first let us go back a little and see the circumstances in which the mutual knowledge of religions has arisen. For the study of religion itself plays a role in bringing cultural diversity to consciousness and so of preparing the way for changes in religious attitudes. It is one of the factors in religious interaction.

It is an elementary, but true, observation that the great period of oriental and anthropological study — the late nineteenth and early twentieth centuries — coincided with the most powerful impact of the West upon non-European cultures. The domination and parcelling up of Africa, the consolidation of the British Raj, the increased penetration of the Middle East, the consolidation of Russia's spread to the Pacific, the missionary and commercial intervention in China, the smashing of American Indian cultures: these were among the great events occurring along the interface between Western and non-Western cultures. It was almost as though the great work of editing alien scriptures, of exploring Indian and Chinese religious history, of beginning the records of tribal societies, the whole enterprise, indeed, of oriental and African and more widely non-European studies — was a mode of compensating for the attempt to Europeanize the world.

At any rate the rough coincidence between the high tide of colonialism and the emergence of the study of religions produced a paradox — on the one hand, Europeanism (by which I include white Americanism), and with it European Christianity, had immense power and had claims to be superior and progressive; on the other hand, the seeds of challenge to the Christian faith were sown in new soil. Nevertheless we have yet to see that challenge fully developed (for it has happened that European theology has been much preoccupied with Western challenges to faith — hence its recent Existentialist flavor). Other forces, it seems, notably Marxism, have intervened to pitch the issues at a different level. But it would incidentally be unwise either to ignore Marxism as a religious force or to overlook the inter-religious changes which are taking place. And to understand these it is necessary to understand what has occurred along the invisible frontier — the interface (as I've called it) between Western and non-Western cultures. Let us call this interface "the white frontier." It is of course not literally a frontier, but rather the margin across which cultural exchanges have taken place.

One type of reaction along the white frontier is illustrated by the history of modern Hinduism. In one respect Hinduism only became Hinduism, a roughly unified ideological system, under the impact of the West. The reshaping of the political and economic structure under the British was accompanied not only by missionary activities and pressures towards certain social reforms but also by the introduction of Western-style higher education. This helped to create a new Hindu intelligentsia which sought to affirm the tradition but in the new circumstance of religious competition. The white frontier itself helped to define the shape of the modern Hindu ideology, which perhaps has had its most effective exponent in Swami Vivekananda, and its most powerful political fruit in the work of Mahatma Gandhi; but has been shaped also by Ram Mohan Roy, Dayananda Sarasvati, Sarvepalli Radhakrishnan and many others.

Since Hinduism has never been a truly missionary religion, and has been in an important sense a congeries of beliefs and practices within a cultural group, the newly reaffirmed Hindu tradition served both a religious and a national function. It had to express both a universal and a national message. The need for the former — the universal message — was simply a result of the configuration of the white frontier. For on the far side of that frontier lay a universal and missionary faith; and the logic of a confrontation with the universal demands a universal riposte: in other words, the growth of a coherent ideology and ethics is not in theory tied to one group only.

We may see this logic by considering what happens when a missionary religion confronts the religious practices and beliefs of a tribal group. Formerly the beliefs of the tribal group were not in competition — it was understood that they were available for initiates. They belonged to a symbolic system of meanings for that particular group: so far the question of affirming them as beliefs true in themselves about which anyone might come to be persuaded had not arisen. They were more like items in a picture in a gallery — not clashing or failing to clash with the items drawn in the different frames of its neighbouring pictures. But once the missionary faith appears on the scene, something has to be said. The riposte "Our beliefs are true but only for us and not in themselves" is essentially unstable. When a powerful person demands that the perspectives of the gallery pictures should cohere, there is a problem.

Something of this situation occurred along the white frontier in India, for though India was multifarious culturally it was (Hindu-wise) in theory ethnic — a tribe writ large. This is not intended as a criticism; if anything the reverse. The

universal and the particular were synthesized by the modern
Hindu ideology, through the claims that all religions point to
the same truth and that the plural Hindu tradition was a
conspicuous working-out of this theory in the laboratory of
India's spirituality. The modern Hindu ideologue was for-
tunate too to be able to draw upon a modified Advaita
Vedanta which corresponded strikingly to the dominant neo-
Hegelianism of late nineteenth century British philosophy.
This reduced the possible tension between the two styles of
religious and educational tradition to which the growing
Indian middle class was unavoidably exposed. In this
manner the white frontier was enabled to run right through
the hearts and minds of the new elite. It is true that this
ideological synthesis has recently been wearing thin: but that
is another story. Although it is worth commenting that it is
hard for the Hindu intellectual to feel now in his bones that
neo-Vedanta corresponds to Western metaphysics, the recent
period has seen a certain partial Indianization of Western
attitudes. The religious pluralism of modern Hindu thinking
(a pluralism guaranteed by a theory of essential unity) was
also adapted to the growing national struggle and found
important practical expression in the essential pacifism of
Gandhi: for Muslim and Hindu in principle were capable of
the same application of truth.

The new Hindu ideology gave a deep ambiguity to Hinduism's relationships with Christianity. There was no reason to
reject Christ's divinity, for manifestations of divinity are
indeed frequent. There were good reasons to develop social
and educational reform along lines pioneered partly by the
Christian missionary. Christian love is noble. Yet somehow
Christianity was threatening, and to many Hindus evil —
partly because it was sometimes used to justify the actions of
a tough, paternal and hard-drinking conquering class, partly
because of its evangelical militancy — highly uncongenial to
a society where the conversion of an individual could wreck
a whole web of family and caste relationships. Often, too,
the attacks upon what the outsider saw as idolatry and super-
stition were looked upon as unfeeling and arrogant. So
hostilities and ambiguities were and still are present in the

Hindu attitude to Christianity.

The logic of Hinduism's newfound universalism has had an effect heralded by Swami Vivekananda's appearance at the famous Parliament of Religions in Chicago in 1893 — 23 years after the foundation of Loyola — namely the beginnings of missions to the West. Here the work of the Ramakrishna mission has been especially important, articulating a Vedanta for the Westerner, often disillusioned with the existing Christian institutions. In this connection I recommend the reading of *What Vedanta means to me*, edited by John Yale — a book with perhaps an unattractive title, but full of biographical evidence of the alienation of religious people from the Christian (mainly the Protestant) tradition. This other-way missionary activity across the white frontier leads us to ask what the future holds in store.

While the drawing of the white frontier has had profound effects on Hinduism, its effects on Buddhism have been varied and only indirectly more dramatic. In Southern and South-East Asia — the lands of the Theravada — Western political penetration was on the whole briefer and less profound. It is time that in Burma and Ceylon the older symbiosis between the Sangha and royal power was destroyed, thus presenting deep problems about the place of Buddhism in the modern state. But Buddhism as a faith has felt itself much less insecure in the face of Western ideas than Hinduism. Various reasons for this can be adduced. First, Buddhism was not nationally tied, having a long and highly successful history of missionary activity. Second, it has generally maintained an ambiguous relationship to popular cults — a kind of coexistence in which the commanding heights of spirituality are occupied by the Order and by the Teaching. Only in principle is this true of Hinduism, and it is no coincidence that Sankara, so influential on the neo-Hindu ideology, was accused of being a crypto-Buddhist. This Buddhist flexibility in relation to the gods provides a means of disengaging and reform, and gives the Buddhist intellectual an assurance of central truths without any need to contradict or destroy his relationships with peasant culture. Third, Buddhism, in not demanding belief in God, could escape the fashionable

critiques of religion influencing many educated Westerners.
The causes of intellectual turmoil in the Victorian world —
evolutionary theory, questions of Biblical historicity, Freudian
psychoanalysis — these have scarcely raised an echo in the
Eastern world. Further, because of the essentially European
character of Marxist theory, there was not the apparent colli-
sion between Marxist atheism and religious belief as was
detectable in the relations between Marxism and Christianity.
Marx attacked Western religion — but did the attack really
apply in the East? Inevitably this was a point of considerable
discussion immediately before the Cultural Revolution in
China.

This has been one, but only one, reason for the search,
in Burma and to some extent elsewhere, for a Buddhist
socialism, as a means of restoring an organic state under
new conditions, to replace the destroyed institutions of the
earlier monarchy.

As far as Theravada Buddhism, in particular, goes, the
reactions along the white frontier have, as I have said, been
undramatic. But quietly the revivification of the Nuddhist
tradition has been promoted; and now increasingly the
Sangha is looking towards the West as a new field of missionary endeavor. The ambiguity towards popular religion,
of which I spoke earlier, characterizes also relations both
to Marxism and Christianity. They are possible elements
to coexist with, so long as the commanding heights are retained. Yet in the case of Christianity, there is from one
point of view an essential incompatibility of belief, which
some Buddhist writers are beginning to stress: ultimately
belief in God cannot be taken seriously, and a Freudian
critique of this belief can be pressed into Buddhist service,
as, for example, in the thinking of K.N. Jayatilleke, the most
penetrating, I suspect, of Theravadin scholars.

It is not hard to see that this nontheistic character of
Buddhism is a main source of its attractions to Westerners
disillusioned with Christian institutions and beliefs. There is
no need to celebrate the death of God in Buddhism.

The effects of the white frontier on China and Japan have,
as we know, been vitally different from their effects in South

and South-East Asia. While in India the white frontier has stimulated reform and the growth of a typically Indian ideology, the Chinese situation has been almost the opposite. In India an Indian theology adapted to face the West was evolved; in China a Western ideology was taken up to solve, by adaptation, the immense problem of social and political disintegration caused in part by Western penetration. China reached across the white frontier and took Marxism; though, as it turned out, only a Chinese version was relevant to the Chinese nationalist task.

The result has been to give Maoism the properties of a national religion — a new Chinese ideology which is essentially as yet not for export. What remains is to see its ultimate relationship to Buddhism, which has been an important contender in the early part of this century for the religious allegiance of Chinese intellectuals. Certainly Tibetan Buddhism has been a prime target of the new ideologists; and traditionally it has been hard for Buddhism to flourish in the absence of a well-established Sangha. Yet perhaps it is because of its evangelical religious properties that Maoism has found it hard to live with other faiths: as it happens, only an evangelical militancy has the human force to change Chinese humanity in the direction of self-sufficient national solidarity, after the disruptions of the first half of the century and the undermining of Chinese stability in the last century.

A third type of reaction along the white frontier is represented by Japan: closing itself up in the nineteenth century in order to exploit the new technologies, developing out of Shinto a religious nationalism, and emerging at Tsu-Shima as an oriental power with as many (and no more) Western properties as were needed to confront the colonial powers as an equal. This pseudo-Westernism paid off until Hiroshima; and even then the occupation could be turned to advantage. And so, in the new era, Japan did not need a Japanese ideology as such, since Japan was set up to look across the white frontier with a certain equanimity born first of military success and then of an unprecedented commercial success. Only in the period of building the industrial power base was nationalistic Shinto important; while now, in the new era of internal change, a whole variety of new religions and religious developments has expressed solutions to problems which are no longer quite along the white frontier, but beyond it. The new religions of Japan are an object lesson to those who facilely see industrialism as a sufficient cause of secularization.

Three types then — the new Indian theology facing West; the new Western theology adapted to Chinese realities; the proliferation of Japanese responses in a nation which altered the white frontier in ways demanded by its own interests.

The world of Islam is not homogeneous; but perhaps, in places, it represents a fourth type of phenomenon along the white frontier. The Islamic heartlands have not been directly subject to systematic colonial rule from the West, due to the long persistence of an ailing Ottoman empire. The penetration of the white frontier into the Middle East has been indirect, on the whole. It is true that north-African Islam, Indian Islam and Indonesian Islam have lived in a colonial situation; but, as with Buddhism, the penetration has been piecemeal and variegated. But the Islamic faith itself has retained a remarkable imperviousness to alien ideologies and religions, and remains therefore a highly significant political force. Indeed it has, despite social changes and the emergence in a number of countries of a cosmopolitan middle class, succeeded in defining a loose alliance of countries — an Islamic commonwealth, so to say. If it has reached across the white frontier, it has been largely to borrow political institutions, intended for adaptation to an overriding Islamic purpose. Turkey, it is true, tried to move right across the frontier; but otherwise the typical Islamic response has been pragmatic rather than theoretical. And Islam retains something of its missionary power, spreading slowly in Africa and contributing to a new stability for societies weakened by foreign and technological forces.

These forces are peculiarly powerful in their effect on the fifth type I wish to draw attention to: tribal societies whose structures are often too rigid to cope with the impact of the West. Sometimes indeed they actually die — for example the last Yahi Indian died in California in 1916. Very often

Christian missionary work has introduced an ethos and a cultus capable of replacing tribal values in the new situation. But in Africa and elsewhere this partial solution does not close the book of changes; and a remarkable consequence is the second great wave of events along the white frontier. I refer to the proliferation of new religious movements: Africanised Christian groups, syncretistic adaptations of parts of Christianity to underlying tribal motifs, new prophetic movements — and so on. An early attempt to describe and evaluate these multitudinous groups and ideas is to be found in Vittorio Lentenari's *The Religions of the Oppressed.* In a way these are smaller versions of the new mass changes in a huge society like China; a new quest for an older identity: new spiritual values to cope with baffling changes from without. Thus, bubbling all the way along the white frontier with tribal societies, are the ferments of new religious movements, in North America, the most conspicuous being Peyotism.

The net result of the phenomena to which I have so sketchily drawn attention is perhaps the opposite of what people might superficially expect. We might expect, in a jet-shrunk world, with much travel and modern communications, a drift towards homogeneity — a new world culture in which the spiritual values of differing traditions are assimilated and synthesized. We tend to think in this way partly because the slogan of unity appeals to us and partly because we only notice the frontier, not what goes on beyond it. For even if the same forces are at work on the hither side of the white frontier, the results of their work depend on what is there on the other side. Every interaction is some sort of synthesis, but the nature of that synthesis varies with the non-European ingredients.

Thus, far from it being the case that world values are converging, there are on the contrary more variations than before (leaving aside the diminution of tribal cultures by total destruction). The new Hindu ideology is added to, and does not displace, the many Hindu systems and practices. New religious movements do not replace Christian denominations, but add to their number. Buddhist socialism is in its own way a new form of Buddhism. Western Vedanta and Californian Zen are new synthetic types of spirituality. Chinese Maoism is a new Marxist religion. So there is no need at all to think that the world becomes less plural by interactions along the white frontier.

I have said little about Christianity, which too has been trying to cope with rapid intellectual and social changes; nor about Humanism and Western Marxism. It may, however, be useful to comment upon one aspect of contemporary Christianity — for it may help to bring out a fallacy in modern diagnoses of the world situation. I refer to modern "secular" Christianity, with Harvey Cox as a major prophet. Here secular Christian man is seen as liberated from traditional religious forms and mythic ways of thinking — a liberation having its genesis in Biblical realism itself. The Christian message and secular hope thus coincide remarkably: and at the same time the problem of other religions is bypassed — from them all should men be liberated. The manpulàtive technological approach to human problems can thus be celebrated in the secular city.

This secular Christianity is fallacious and rests upon a lack of realism about the way men are and the way the world is. It is fallacious for a number of reasons relevant to our theme. First, because it supposes that technology imposes a *unique* solution upon social life: so that a homogeneous world culture is necessary to the solving of the problems of economic development. But this supposition is highly questionable, to put it mildly, and based on slender and selective experience of white industrialization. Second, it supposes that Western values are identical with secular values — and thus is merely a new affirmation of European missionary enterprise, with a *carte blanche* for undermining and destroying alien religions. Third, it neglects the cultural dimension of human feelings: it is not sufficient for a person to attain personal liberation — not that this can usually be achieved: the secular frontier merely throws up new forms of religion on the other side, but he must be organically connected with his social environment. This, indeed, is central to the understanding of all the phenomena to which I have been drawing attention. In them all we perceive an attempt to recreate or preserve that which has been challenged and threatened by the forces streaming across the white frontier.

I do not deny that a certain homogeneity of outlook has spread across many of the world's middle class; and since this class is the midwife of intellectuals it is easy to think that a drift to unity is occurring. But let us notice that this incipient homogeneity has a special cause — that nearly all modern educational systems, notably universities, are built on the Western model and tend to be imbued with a similar kind of rationalism. But this itself, though it may lead to a thinly spread cosmopolitanism, is not ultimately as significant a factor as at first sight may appear — since a rationalist cosmopolitanism is no basis for articulating the problems of a given culture and so in the long run proves uninfluential and ineffective. It merely contributes to an *extra* culture superimposed on those of the world: a rationalist cosmopolitan noosphere, so to say.

I would argue then that an increase, rather than a decrease, of religious and ideological pluralism is what characterizes the modern world. I have treated this theme in terms of the white frontier, for this has been so influential in the colonial and post-colonial period. But it has to be remembered that this is only one of many possible interfaces: the exchanges across these other frontiers may well be accelerated in the years to come. In any event, the period of white expansion may soon be at an end.

I have discussed this chain of reactions without reference to the truth or worth of these religious and ideological developments. But a pluralistic world is bound to pose acutely questions of belief and choice. The increasing consciousness of diversity and the abandonment of a facile diagnosis of man's unitary destiny is bound to call in question our own commitments and values. It may be that this will make some people too eclectic and too relativist: but on the whole there is much to learn by looking from the other direction across the white frontier, before it disappears to be replaced by many other frontiers.

It would be flying in the face of history to suppose that

the result of a conscious pluralism leads to a simple syncretism. Christianity, for example, is not going to wither or change its shape entirely by living beside Buddhism. But a lot can be learned by seeing deeply into other men's values and concerns. This is a major function of the history of religions — to perform fruitful introductions.

Thus the hopeful side of increasing pluralism is that it occurs in a general context where communication is more feasible than ever before; and with luck we may look forward to a world which is neither homogeneous nor totally ignorant of our mutual differences. There is thus no *single* evolution of men's values. But it may be that a meta-value (so to say) will become more and more vital — the higher value of living reasonably peaceably with those of other commitments, and so eschewing the unrealistic temptation to treat other men in our own image. I think it is also a consequence of what I have been trying to say that the truth, to make us free, must be emotionally and culturally acceptable: for the living truth is not just about facts, but about responses and values too.

PART II

VALUES AND THE SOCIAL SCIENCES

Prices and Values: Infinite Worth in a Finite World

Kenneth E. Boulding

I am going to take advantage of the fact that I do earn my living by being an economist by introducing a few technological concepts at the beginning, though I want to keep the technical part to a minimum. The main theme of this essay is the contribution of economics to the general theory of value, and particularly to the theory of ethical choice and personal identity. In order to make these applications, however, it is necessary to look first at some basic concepts of economics itself.

A central concern of economic theory has been the "theory of value," which is the theory of what determines the relative prices of commodities. This theory turns out to have broad application to all problems involving choice, whether economic, political, or moral. The first basic concept of the theory is that of a transformation ratio. If A is transformed into B, the transformation ratio is how many units of B can be obtained by giving up one unit of A. Transformation is a common phenomenon in all fields of life, and it is not surprising therefore that transformation ratios are very important quantities. In exchange, for instance, we are giving up one thing and acquiring another, and the transformation here is the ratio of exchange, that is, how many units of what we get do we receive for each unit of what we give up. If one of the things exchanged is money, then the transformation ratio, or the ratio of exchange, becomes the price. If butter is 80 cents a pound, this means that by going to a place where butter is sold, I can give up 80 cents and get a pound of butter, or

31

give up 160 cents and get two pounds and so on.

In production the transformation ratio is a marginal cost. If a farmer, for instance, must give up a dollar's worth altogether in cash, raw materials, seed, depreciation of machinery and so on, in order to get a bushel of wheat, then the marginal cost of the wheat is a dollar a bushel. The cost concept in general is a transformation concept. It implies that we have to give up certain things in order to get other things. In processes of production these may be expressed in physical transformation ratios. For instance, how much wheat must I give up if I grind it into a bushel of flour? As a more general concept, economists have developed notions of alternative costs. If we refrain from producing an automobile, for instance, how many tons of wheat can we eventually produce with the resources that this will release?

The relative price structure would be the set of exchange ratios, or transformations in exchange, of each commodity for every other. This enormous list can be simplified somewhat if we express the price of all commodities in terms of a common unit called a numeraire, which is usually money, though it could theoretically be anything. Thus, if butter exchanges for 80 cents a pound, and bread for 10 cents a pound, we know that a pound of butter will exchange for eight pounds of bread.

Economists have always argued that the relative price structure is not arbitrary, and that there is a "normal" price structure which is determined roughly by the structure of alternative costs at those levels of output which satisfy the structure of demand. Then if the actual structure of relative prices in the market at which things are actually exchanging differs from the normal price structure some commodities will be underpriced and their production will decline and some will be overpriced and their production will increase. This will lower the prices of the overpriced commodities and raise the prices of the underpriced commodities, and so move the whole structure of market prices towards the normal price structure. This is classical price theory as it was developed essentially in the first instance by Adam Smith. The normal price structure may indeed be a range rather than a particular set of relative prices, but the validity of the concept can hardly be questioned, that is, there is some set or range of prices outside of which we get into some kind of trouble, in the shape of surpluses or shortages of commodities, even though these surpluses and shortages may be perpetuated indefinitely by some form of grants or coercion.

The principal changes in the normal price structure in the last one or two hundred years have been the result mainly of relative changes in the technology of production of different commodities. Thus, the price of bread has been declining very sharply relative to education, mainly because there has been a great technical improvement in wheat production, whereas education is an unprogressive, perhaps even a retrogressive, industry in which there has been very little real technical change and virtually no cost reduction. When I get up to lecture, this is almost exactly what Plato was doing twenty-five hundred years ago, at least in regard to the form of the activity. Thus, we see a constant change in the normal price structure with a fall in the relative price of most things in which technical improvement is taking place and a rise in the relative price of those things in which there is little technical improvement.

Consumer preferences, that is, the structure of demand, have some influence on the normal price structure, both as they affect the willingness to supply factors of production and as they affect relative outputs, but these influences tend to be of the second order of magnitude and can be neglected for the purpose of this essay. It is important to note, however, that transformation ratios can be used to describe a preference structure or a set of choice values. We have in economics a concept called the rate of indifference substitution, which is how much of one commodity I can substitute for one unit of another without feeling any worse off. If I do not care whether I have 10 more nuts and 1 less orange, then I have a rate of indifference substitution of 10 nuts per orange. This is one useful way of describing subjective value. We could call this the compensation principle, that is, we measure the value of something by what we would have to receive in order to compensate us for giving it up. In its extreme form this is the principle that every man has his price, even though the price on occasion may be very high or even infinite. If we have a given market price structure, there is a tendency for people to adjust the quantity of goods possessed, produced, or consumed, so that the price structure corresponds to the rate of indifference substitution. If the amount of nuts and oranges in my possession is such that my rate of indifference substitution is 10 nuts per orange, and in the market I can get 12 nuts for an orange, then I would be motived to exchange oranges for nuts, until the rate of substitution conforms to the rate of exchange. This is a rather technical point which will be familiar to economists, but it has very wide implications.

I pointed out in an earlier article[1] how these concepts of the economic theory of value can be extended to illuminate the problem of ethical choice. Wherever choice is involved, whether between nuts and oranges, or between liberty and justice, the theory of relative value is relevant. We have to look both at technical and at the psychological transformation ratios in order to see what is going to determine the "ethical market." On the technical or the supply side, we have to ask ourselves, for instance, how much liberty can we get if we give up so much justice, or how much justice can we get if we give up so much liberty? This is a problem in social technology and like all technology it may change over time. Then on the demand side we have to ask ourselves how much justice are we willing to give up for so much liberty. The actual choices in this case, for instance, choices in regard to political systems which people make, are a result of the interaction of their perception of the social technology on the one hand and their psychological preferences on the other.

A few interesting principles emerge from the analysis. One is that the scarcity of anything tends to produce a high subjective valuation, that is, if we perceive something as scarce, we are willing to give up a good deal of what we perceive as plentiful in order to get a unit of what we perceive as scarce. If by technology, either social or physical, we diminish the scarcity we may diminish the relative subjective value. A fundamental proposition which noneconomists often do not understand is that transformation or valuation coefficients, both in costs and technology on the one hand and in subjective valuation on the other, are variables not constants. They vary, in particular with how much of various things you have. They also depend on each other and interact with each other. The one thing we cannot assume in the structure of relative means in any sense is invariance of values, particularly with regard to the quantities of things which are valued.

Thus, I sometimes think that the high value which we ostensibly place on love in Western society is a result of its scarcity. Historically we have been a rather loveless society. We have treated children roughly and emphasized virtues such as productivity and aggressiveness. It is not surprising, therefore, that we give love a very high value because we have so little of it.

Another very important conclusion of this analysis which is familiar to economists is that small differences in preferences may lead to large differences in the position which is actually preferred. The equilibrium of choice, that is to say, may be precarious in the sense that a fairly small change in the underlying conditions may lead to large changes in the positions actually preferred. This is a little disconcerting to orderly-minded people, but it is frequently true. In many systems which are like this, small causes can produce large effects, and large causes can produce small effects. This is the type of phenomenon which is highly characteristic of ecological systems and I would argue very strongly that systems of preference and of morality are essentially ecological systems within the field of man's cognitive structure.

An ecological system is one in which we have a number of populations of different kinds, each one of which has an equilibrium position which depends on the size of all the others. Sometimes a quite small change in the underlying conditions can produce a greatly different set of species or "ecosystem." Illinois, before the coming of the American, provided a striking example of this principle, for it was here that the boundary between the forests and the prairie was found. On one side of this boundary the dominant ecosystem was the forest and on the other side were the grasslands with almost a completely different set of species of plants and animals. At the boundary, however, the difference in the underlying conditions was very small. A slight increase in rainfall might produce the forests, a slight decrease, the prairie.

There is rather similar phenomenon in society. We have clusters or ecosystems of values and preferences just as we have clusters and ecosystems of species of plants and animals. The ideas and the practices that inhabit the dry grassy prairie of Unitarianism are extremely different from those that inhabit the lush forest of the Jesuits. Nevertheless, the underlying circumstances which make the difference may actually differ very little, and this small difference in the underlying conditions may create a very large difference in the final social species which results. We are often unwilling to recognize this phenomenon, particularly if we build our identities around the particular social system that we have to inhabit, so we like to think of the differences between us and our competing social systems as very large, as indeed in terms of observable ideas and practices they may be. The difference in the underlying conditions, however, may be quite small.

Another possible contribution of economics to the general theory of value and ethical choice is the large body of literature known as welfare economics. I have to confess that I think there is much less in this body of literature than meets the eye, but it is extremely good for passing examinations with, it can be taught, and professors can find out whether students have learned it, which is one thing that makes it survive in the academic community. Nevertheless, it is based on an assumption which seems to me so remote from reality that its conclusions are highly suspect, or at least have to be very fundamentally modified. Its basic assumption is that people are selfish, that is, that their estimate of their own welfare depends only on the particular set of commodities which they happen to possess or enjoy, and is independent of their perception of the welfare of other people. The same assumption underlies the concept of the Paretian optimum, named after its formulator, Vilfredo Pareto. This is any set of conditions of the social system in which it is not possible to make somebody better off without also making somebody worse off. As long as it is possible to make somebody better off without making anybody worse off, the Paretian optimum has not been reached.

This concept has at least the virtue of pointing out that there are many conditions of society in which bargains or other movements are possible which do not involve real conflict in the sense of somebody getting worse off and somebody else getting better off. Nevertheless, it is unsatisfactory as a general social optimum because it neglects the possibility of malevolence or benevolence, that is, situations in which perceived utilities are related. A persona may be defined as benevolent if his contemplation of an increase in the welfare of another increases his own welfare. Malevolence is simply negative benevolence, that is, when the contemplation of an increase in the welfare of another decreases one's own welfare. These are highly characteristic conditions of human beings. One can argue indeed that selfishness, defined as indifference to the welfare of another, is actually very rare and represents, as it were, merely the zero point on the scale of malevolence-benevolence. Benevolence and malevolence can be measured, at least subjectively, by the concept of the rate of benevolence, which is how much a person would sacrifice in order to perceive that another person is better off by a dollar. Selfishness than represents zero rate of benevolence, malevolence is a negative rate of benevolence. If, for instance, it has been costing us about four dollars to do one dollar's worth of damage to the North Vietnamese, as seems to have been approximately the case in 1969, our rate of benevolence towards them is -4.

We cannot understand the social system at all without taking account of some structure of malevolence and benevolence. Without a moderate degree of benevolence, for instance, community of any kind would be virtually impossible. Even exchange requires modest degrees of benevolence for it is very hard to legitimate exchange without it, except in its most primitive form, such as the "silent trade" between tribes with a degree of malevolence towards each other. Commercial and mercantile society, however, cannot be established unless there is a moderate degree of benevolence among its members. Even when we go to the store and buy a shirt, which is a very abstract relationship, we smile at the clerk; we pass the time of day, we do not at least create an atmosphere of hostility. The little courtesies and politenesses indeed which sometimes, especially to the high-minded, appear as mere frills and excrescences of society, have in fact a crucial function of creating and sustaining a minimum of benevolence which is necessary to legitimate exchange and almost any kind of human intercourse. Beyond a certain rate of benevolence society tends to fall apart, or else the malevolence has to be ritualized in legal or military conflict. Fortunately, it is quite easy to put malevolence and benevolence into economies by an extension of existing techniques. There is no reason at all for economists to make the absurdly unrealistic assumption that everybody is selfish.

Another grave weakness of welfare economics, and indeed of a great deal of economic theory, is the assumption that individual preferences are given and are not subject to orderly change. This is the doctrine that is literally for the birds. The preferences of birds, which are often quite strong, are mostly genetic in origin, though even birds have to learn a little, for instance, the finer points of singing, after they have hatched. On the whole, however, the strong preferences which orioles have for other orioles and oriole nests and their lack of preference for robins and robins' nests is built in by their genetic structure. Birds have a great deal of race prejudice but they do not seem to learn this from their parents. In the case of man, however, even though we do have some preferences of genetic origin at birth — we like milk, we like being dry, we like warmth, we like mother or some reasonable substitute, and we do not like being wet, cold, hungry and insecure — beyond that, all our values are learned in the course of life and everything else is added on to us. If at the age of maturity we like or do not like caviar, raw fish or transubstantiation, these are preferences that we have learned on the way.

This is why we have to be extremely careful in applying

to man the things that we learn from the study of animal behavior. Animal ethology is fine for geese and rats, but it is not necessarily applicable to humans, mainly because the most extraordinary thing about the human organism is that what we have at birth is potential and very little else. Every new baby is a bit like an immigrant going into Kansas. He has a great plain of potential in front of him and he fills this and settles it with the farms and the cities that he builds from his experience. These plains of potential, of course, have some contours. There are genetic limits on the human learning process and there are people who seem genetically to have greater aptitudes for certain specific things than others. Nevertheless, I am sure that the human organism at birth is much more like Kansas than like Colorado. The individual may be faced with certain "river valleys" and easy ways and hard ways to go that are genetically based, such as musical ability which in the extreme case is going to be hard for the tone deaf, or perhaps even mathematical ability. On the whole, however, I suspect that the genetic base for human learning consists of limits which for most people are so far off that we don't have to worry about them.

On the whole, therefore, we have to understand adult values by looking at the learning processes by which they are produced. There is a very fundamental principle, both in biological growth and in social systems, which I have called D'Arcy Thompson's Law, in honor of the famous biologist who wrote *On Growth and Form*. As I state it, it is simply that everything is the way it is because it got that way. In order to understand being, we have to understand becoming, particularly in the case of the human being — we are what we are because of the life history that we have gone through up to date, because of what we did, because of things that happened to us, and because of the inputs and outputs of information and also the internally generated inputs and outputs. One of the most remarkable things about the human body is that it is capable of this enormous flood of internal messages that we call the imagination, and this contributes enormously to the learning process.

In any kind of dynamic theory, therefore, we have to

assume that values, that is, internal preferences, are a major element in determining the direction in which our images of the world develop, and yet these internal values themselves are learned. The trouble is we do not know how they are learned. Education, not excepting religious education, is still, to a very large extent, a shot in the dark. Education, that is, is still a craft industry. It has as yet benefited very little from the development of scientific knowledge about human learning, simply because there is so little scientific knowledge about human learning. Craft industries, of course, represent a degree of real skill and knowledge and often produce very nice things. Even in education, therefore, we must have been doing something right, otherwise we would never have been able to transmit cultures from one generation to the next to get to the point where we are today. Nevertheless, craft industries tend to produce expensive things and education is no exception. We are producing something, but we really do not have very much idea how we do it, and even less idea how to improve what we are doing.

Another weakness of economics, which is also a weakness of social science in general, is the assumption that the actor is invariant with regard to action. A great deal of social science indeed almost seems to study action in the absence of any actor at all, which we might almost call the study of the no-person group. In psychology the actor is frequently regarded merely as an intervening variable, especially in behaviorism. In economic theory there are no real actors at all, only flows of money and commodities and other exchangeables between the nodes of the network. There are no real people in it at all, only transformers of input into output.

There is some excuse for this neglect of people because they are appallingly complicated and if we try to bring them into the social sciences it tends to mess them up. Nevertheless, at some point or other we have to sneak people back in, simply because there are some types of behavior and patterns in the social system which are actor-related.

I am prepared to admit that in what we usually think of as economic behavior, as directed by cost-benefit analysis, the actor may often be taken as a given invariant and therefore is irrelevant. In most cost-benefit analyses it does not matter very much who does the calculations or even who will get the benefits or who will pay the costs, as long as both costs and benefits can be evaluated in some common unit, such as the dollar. A good deal of human behavior, not only what we ordinarily think of as economic behavior in the market, but also political, marital and even religious behavior, follows this kind of pattern.

Nevertheless, I have argued that there is another kind of behavior of which we must take account if we are to understand human life and experience which I have called heroic behavior, though I am not sure whether this is a good name for it. This is behavior which is "identity-originating," that is, which is perceived as a necessary output from the kind of person that we perceive ourselves to be. This is "doing your own thing" in the language of the hippies. This is doing what you do because you are what you are. As I have observed elsewhere[2] there are three major forms of heroic behavior — the sporting, the military, and the religious. The risks and the agonies which people go through in the name of sport are difficult to explain unless we introduce the urge for the heroic. Otherwise it is hard to explain uncomfortable and dangerous occupations, like skiing, playing hockey and climbing mountains. Mallory is reported to have said that he climbed Mt. Everest "because it was there." This seems like a totally inadequate explanation. Mountains will stay there whether we climb them or not. Even though I have to confess that I am neither a sportsman nor an athlete, and indeed generally repress the impulse to take exercise, I also have to confess that I climbed Long's Peak in Colorado at the age of 59, which was very hard work, so there is clearly something about mountains which brings out a preposterous urge for the heroic and that upsets all rational economic behavior.

We see the same phenomenon in military behavior, of which perhaps *The Charge of the Light Brigade* is the most famous — "Their's not to reason why, their's but to do and die." Anybody doing cost-benefit analysis would probably not be in the Light Brigade at all, and would certainly not have charged.

Similarly, I would argue that religion also cannot be understood, at least as a human phenomenon, without introducing the concept of heroic behavior. There is, of course, a certain amount of mercenary religion (How much do we have to pay to get off so many days in purgatory?), just as there are mercenary soldiers, but if all religion had been economic it would never have had the immense impact on the human mind and on human behavior which it has had. The prophets and the saints, especially, are essentially heroic in their behavior in the sense that they do what they do because of what they conceive themselves to be. The real saint gives and does not count the cost, labors and asks for no reward, even in heaven, because it is part of the image of the self. In Christian terms this is the "new man" in Christ which is "put on," (Ephesians 4:24). Behavior in the saint then arises out of the perception of a new personal identity.

Personal identities, however, cannot simply be taken for granted. They have to be selected, sustained, and expanded. This is a rare form of human behavior, yet it is so significant in explaining other behavior that it must be added, for if behavior arises out of a perception of identity, then we have to ask ourselves how does the identity itself arise out of human behavior? What we "are" is not merely given to us by genetics or by chance; it often has to be chosen. It is not enough to "be"; we often have to ask ourselves, "Should we be something else?" The question of what we are not is often just as important as the question of what we are. We cannot fully understand human life and behavior without understanding a phenomenon like conversion, that is, identity change. Identity change is not of course always desirable. Sometimes a person changes his identity in a pathological direction, as we see in the extreme cases of schizophrenics. On the other end of the scale we also have identities which change towards the supernormal and hence become sources of evolutionary potential.

Identity change towards the supernormal is crucial to the understanding of human history. I have scandalized some sociologists by urging them to consider revelation as perhaps the most important single phenomenon in the social system, even in terms of pure secular theory. In this secular sense a revelation is the creation of evolutionary potential, often through the development of some supernormal identity. Evolutionary potential is a potential for the creation of a "phylum," whether biological or social. As de Chardin points out, the great phyla of human history, whether these are religions or nations, or even the scientific community, always originate in some creation of evolutionary potential. Sometimes this is perceived by those who participate in the events of revelation. Sometimes it happens so quietly and imperceptibly through the contributions of many different people that it is not perceived as a new phylum for a long time. Even in the case when a revelation is perceived it is often perceived only by a small group who are often dismissed by the world around them as visionaries. I have indeed a kind of litany which goes "Who would have thought at the time" — that, for instance, an old man with a beard in the British Museum in the middle of the nineteenth century would have caused so much uproar in the twentieth, or that a camel driver in Arabia would have established a great civilization stretching from Spain to the Philippines, or that the son of a carpenter's wife in an obscure and despised town on the edge of the Roman Empire would have set in motion a chain of events which would have produced a celebration in Chicago, almost two thousand years later. All conceptions are indeed mysterious, whether immaculate or not. Information processes do not penetrate into them. Evolutionary theory always leads us to be wise only after the event. And yet there is no form of human behavior of such crucial importance as that which creates evolutionary potential.

Perhaps we can reconcile the three forms of behavior which we now might perhaps identify as economic, heroic and revelationary, if we think of the person as a moral asset and ask ourselves what increases the net moral worth. The concept of net moral worth is one of these difficult, vague, but nevertheless essential concepts. It always tends to escape exact definition, quantification, and there are always important elements in it which escape our information system. Nevertheless, even if something cannot be known exactly, this does not mean that it is not important. In fact, important things are often apt to be inaccessible to exact knowledge. In spite of the epistemological difficulties, therefore, I venture to put forth the proposition that the increase of net moral worth is the highest priority objective of human life and society, even at the secular level. In order to implement this proposition, however, we need to know much more than we do about the production functions of net moral worth, that is, what inputs and outputs of the person in fact increase his net moral worth. All actual measures of worth are only substitutes, such as for instance the net accounting worth, and the relation between these and the net moral worth is highly nonlinear, although it is not random. Thus, even in accounting terms the destitute man often has a lower moral worth in his own estimation than in the estimation of everybody else, and the rich often tend to have a high moral worth, at least in their own estimation. It has been an important function of religion, however, to point out that these relations at least are very loose and may easily be reversed, as in the famous case of Dives and Lazarus.

If now we take the increase of net moral worth as the prime objective of life and society, what does it imply for education, for welfare, for defense and for religion? The education that destroys the identity of a child, for instance, that teaches him that he is "no good," which all so often happens in the ghettos and on Indian reservations, and is apt to happen in all "colonial" situations, is a moral disaster. To destroy the identity of a child indeed comes as close to being a sin against the Holy Ghost as one can imagine. Nevertheless, we are always in danger of this in formal education because we learn only by making mistakes and yet the reaction to making mistakes if they are corrected in the wrong spirit, is often not learning (I made a mistake, but I will not have to do it again.), but is the destruction of identity (I made a mistake and I will always make mistakes.). We face much the same problem in our welfare system. The "cold" charity that is such an utter debasement of love is destructive of the identity both of the recipient and of the donor and perpetuates the very evil which it is intended to correct.

It is defense which perhaps presents the most acute moral dilemmas of our day. A defense which destroys the moral worth of what is defended is clearly worthless and we see too often a kind of defense which does destroy what is defended, because the acts done in defense destroy the moral worth of the defender. How can people go on loving their country when their country does such unspeakable things in the cause of its own defense? The use of napalm and defoliants in Vietnam has probably done much more damage to the United States than it has done to the people it was used against, because it has undermined our own sense of our own moral worth and has reinforced the moral worth of our "enemies." This dilemma of defense is by no means confined to the national state. We find it in the individual person — "For what shall it profit a man if he shall gain the whole world and lose his own soul?" (Mark 8:36). We find it also in religion which can all too easily destroy itself by the unholy alliances which it makes in its own defense.

The origins of religion as we know are multitudinous and not infrequently disreputable, like the origins of most things. It has origins in fear and deception, in exploitation and in magic. Nevertheless, it cannot be understood as a phenomenon in human history without seeing it in the first place as a heroic enterprise which arises ultimately out of a vision of infinite worth. The vision of infinite worth, of course, is always being wrecked on the rocks of the finite world. We have to live in a finite world of scarcity and economics and it is hard to sustain a vision of infinite worth in a world of such finitude. Nevertheless, it is a goal that justifies the direction and the direction which justifies the goal. The finite translation of the vision of infinite worth is in the direction of constant increase of moral value. We do not know the "omega point," as de Chardin calls it. I have no claims to know the secrets of the universe, but I do need to know which way is "up" and I have a good deal of confidence that "up" is in the direction of the increase of net moral worth, and that this is related to increase in the valuation of the person in his own eyes and in the eyes of those around him.

Almost everyone has a phrase which has gone with them

all through their life. One of these which has been important to me is from George Fox, the founder of the Society of Friends, who urged people to "walk cheerfully over the world, answering that of God in everyone." The idea that it is possible to see in every person that we meet an element of infinite worth and to answer and respond to, this seems to me the way that each of us grows, and as each of us grows we all grow. This it seems to me is what even economics is all about. All commodities, after all, are only intermediate goods. The ultimate product of economics is people of high moral worth. Unless it produces these, the whole system is worthless. And unless we have some vision of infinite moral worth, we tend to reach an equilibrium and be satisfied with what we have achieved.

Endnotes

1. K. E. Boulding: "Some Contributions of Economics to the General Theory of Value," *Philosophy of Science* 23, 1 (Jan. 1956), 1-14.
2. K. E. Boulding: "Economics as a Moral Science," *American Economic Review* (March 1969), pp. 1-12.

Insiders and Outsiders: An Essay in the Sociology of Knowledge

Robert K. Merton

The sociology of knowledge is widely recognised as a complex and estoeric subject, remote from the urgent problems of contemporary social life. To some of us, it seems quite the other way.[1] Especially in times of great social change, precipitated by social conflict and attended by much cultural disorganization, the perspectives provided by the sociology of knowledge bear directly upon problems agitating the society. For it is then that differences in the values, commitments and modes of thought of conflicting groups become deepened into cleavages. Intellectual orientations once held in common become fragmented. An active and reciprocal distrust between groups finds expression in intellectual perspectives which are no longer located in the same universe of discourse. The more deepseated the mutual distrust, the more does the argument of the other appear so palpably implausible or absurd that one no longer inquires into substance or logical structure in order to assess its validity. Instead, one confronts the argument with an entirely different question: how does it happen to be advanced at all? Thought thus becomes altogether functionalized, interpreted only in terms of its social or economic or psychological sources and functions. In the political forum, this involves reciprocated attacks on the integrity of the opponent; in the academic arena, it leads to reciprocal ideological analyses. In both, the process feeds upon and nourishes collective insecurities.

Within this context, we come upon the renewed contemporary relevance of a longstanding problem in the sociology of knowledge: the problem of patterned differentials among social groups and strata in access to certain types of knowledge. In its strong form, the claim is put forward as a matter of epistemological principle that particular groups have monopolistic access to particular knowledge. In the weaker, more empirical form, the claim holds that these groups have privileged access with other groups also being able to acquire that knowledge but at greater cost.

Claims of this general sort have been periodically introduced. For one imposing example, Marx, a progenitor of the sociology of knowledge as of much else in social thought, advanced the argument that one social class in particular was strategically located in capitalistic society to obtain a valid understanding of its development. For a considerably less imposing example, the national-socialist (Nazi) theoretician, Ernst Krieck, expressed an entire ideology in contrasting the access to authentic scientific knowledge by men of unimpeachable Aryan ancestry with the corrupt versions of such knowledge available to non-Aryans.[2] For our purposes, we need not review the array of elitist theories that have laid claim to social differentials in access to new knowledge. Differing in detail, the doctrines are alike in distinguishing between Insider access to knowledge and Outsider exclusion from it.

A version of the doctrine in this country has lately been put forward by some militant black intellectuals. In its strong form, the argument holds that, as a matter of social epistemology, *only* black historians can truly understand black history, only black ethnologists can understand black culture, only black sociologists can understand the social life of blacks, and so on. In its weaker form, some practical concessions are made. With regard to programs of Black Studies, for example, it is proposed that some white professors of the relevant subjects might be brought in since there are not yet enough black scholars to man all the proliferating programs of study. But as Professor Nathan Hare, the self-styled militant black sociologist states, this is only on temporary and conditional sufferance: "Any white professors involved in the program would have to be black in spirit in order to last. The same is true for 'Negro' professors."[3] Apart from this limited concession, it is maintained that there is a body of black history, black psychology, black ethnology, black politics and black sociology which can be significantly advanced only by black scholars and social scientists.

In its fundamental character, this represents a major claim in the sociology of knowledge, a claim to the ultimate balkanization of social science, with separate baronies exclusively in the hands of Insiders. Generalizing the specific claim somewhat, it would appear to follow that if only black scholars can understand blacks, then only white scholars can understand whites. Generalizing further from race to nation, that only French scholars can understand French society and, of course, with Americans alone being capable of understanding Americans. Once generated by the composite principle of group solipsism and collective subjectivism, the list of Insider claims to monopoly of knowledge becomes indefinitely expansible to all manner of social formations. Only youth become capable of understanding youth (just as, presumably, only the middle-aged are able to understand their age peers). So, proletarians alone understand proletarians and presumably capitalists, capitalists; only Catholics, Catholics; Jews, Jews and to halt the inventory of socially atomized claims to knowledge with a case that on its face seems to have some merit, with plainly only sociologists being able to understand their fellow sociologists.

The claim that a monopoly of knowledge about groups is vested in their members appears to be a doctrine of group solipsism and group soliloquy, with no possibility of effective communication across boundaries. The claim can be put in the vernacular with no great loss of meaning: you have to be one in order to understand one. In somewhat less idiomatic language, it can be described as the doctrine of the Insider.

The Insider is presumably one who has special access to knowledge merely by virtue of his group membership or social position. In certain universes of discourse, the concept appears in the form of a question-begging pun: Insider as

Insighter, one endowed with insight into matters obscure to others, having penetrating discernment and understanding. Once adopted, the pun provides a specious solution of the problem but the serious Insider doctrine has its own rationale.

Before going on to examine the intricacies of that argument, we must note that sociologically there is nothing fixed about the lines separating Insiders from Outsiders. As situations involving different values arise, the lines of separation change. For a large number of white Americans, Joe Louis was a member of an outgroup. But when Louis defeated the nazified Max Schmeling, many of these same white Americans acclaimed him as a member of the (national) in-group. National self-esteem took precedence over racial separatism. That redefinitions of group boundaries are situationally determined in the realm of the intellect as well is the point of Albert Einstein's ironic observation in an address at the Sorbonne: "If my theory of relativity is proven successful, Germany will claim me as a German and France will declare that I am a citizen of the world. Should my theory prove untrue, France will say I am a German and Germany will declare that I am a Jew."[4]

The claim that only Insiders can understand the history, social life and culture of a group ignores this matter of shifting group boundaries as we shall see in examining its rationale. We can quickly pass over the trivial version of the rationale: the argument that the Outsider may be incompetent, that he may be given to quick and superficial forays into the culture he studies or that he may not even know the language of the group he is observing. That this sort of incompetence can be found is beyond doubt, but it holds no principled interest for us. Foolish men or badly trained men are to be found everywhere and anthropologists and sociologists and psychologists and historians engaged in study of groups other than their own surely have their fair share of them. But such cases do not bear on the Insider principle. For that principle does not refer to stupidly designed and stupidly executed inquiries that happen to be made by stupid Outsiders; it asserts a far more fundamental position. According to the doctrine of the Insider, the Outsider, no matter how careful and talented he may be, is excluded in principle from gaining access to the social and cultural truth.

The doctrine holds that the Outsider has a structurally imposed incapacity to comprehend alien cultures and societies. Unlike the Insider, he has not had the run of experience that makes up life in the group and so he cannot have the direct, intuitive sensitivity that alone makes empathic understanding possible. It is argued that only through continued socialization in the life of a group can one become fully aware of the symbolisms and realities of the group, only so can one empathically understand the fine-grained meanings of behavior, feelings and aspirations, only so can one decipher the unwritten grammar of conduct and the nuances of cultural idiom. Or, in the words of Ralph W. Conant, "whites are not and never will be as sensitive to the black community precisely because they are not part of that community."[5]

The thesis has a degree of plausibility and far-reaching implications. That the dominant white society has long imposed social barriers which excluded Negroes from full participation in the society is a tragic commonplace of history. But what has not been typically noticed by whites is that the high walls of segregation did not at all separate whites and blacks symmetrically from intimate observation of the social life of the other. For generations, as socially invisible men and women, Negroes at work in white enclaves moved around the walls of segregation to discover what was on the other side. The highly visible whites, in contrast, characteristically did not want to find out about life in the Negro community and could not even in those rate cases where they would. The structure of racial segregation meant that those whites who prided themselves on understanding Negroes could know their stylized role behaviors in relation to whites but next to nothing of their private lives. Thus, segregation made for asymmetrical sensitivities across the divide.

A somewhat less stringent rationale for the Insider doctrine maintains only that Insider and Outsider scholars have substantially different foci of attention. The argument goes somewhat as follows. The Insider, sharing the concerns and problems of the group or at the least being in a position to become thoroughly aware of them, will so direct his inquiries as to have them be relevant to those concerns. The Outsider will inquire into problems relevant to his own distinctive values and interests. These are bound to differ from those of the group under study if only because he occupies a different place in the social structure.

This is an hypothesis which has the not unattractive quality of being subject to empirical investigation. It should be possible to compare the spectrum of research problems about, say, the Negro population in this country which have been investigated by Negro and by white sociologists to see whether the foci of attention in fact differ and if so, in which respects. The only inquiry of this kind I happen to know of was published a quarter of a century ago.[6] William Fontaine found that Negro scholars tended to adopt analytical rather than morphological categories in their study of behavior, that they emphasized environmental rather than biological determinants of that behavior and tended to make use of strikingly dramatic rather than representative data. All this was ascribed to a caste-induced resentment among Negro scholars. But since this lone study failed to examine the frequency of comparable subjects and categories among white scholars of the time, its findings are somewhat less than compelling. All the same, the questions it addressed remain. For there is theoretical reason to suppose that the foci of research attention among Insiders and Outsiders and perhaps even their categories of analysis will tend to differ. At least to the extent that social location affects the selection of problems for investigation, as Max Weber's notion of *Wertbeziehung* suggests it does, the spectrum of problems will vary.

Unlike the stringent rationale which maintains that Insiders and Outsiders will arrive at different (and presumably contradictory) results even when they do examine the same problems, this weaker rationale argues only that they will simply talk past one another. Combining the two rationales, the extended version of the Insider doctrine can also be put in the vernacular: one must not only be one in order to understand one; one must be one in order to understand what is most worth understanding.

By this point, it must be evident that the doctrine of the Insider is linked up with what Sumner long ago described as ethnocentrism: the conviction that one's group is the center of things. Often enough, this is joined with the belief that one's group is superior to all cognate groups, whether nation, class, race, region or organization. This can be seen in a series of studies of what Theodore Caplow has called the aggrandizement effect: the distortion upwards of the prestige of a group or organization by its members.[7] In his study of 33 different types of organizations — ranging from dance studios to Protestant and Catholic churches, from Skid Row missions to big banks, and from advertising agencies to university departments — Caplow found that members overestimated the prestige of their organization some eight times as often as they underestimated it (as compared with judgments by outsiders). More decisively, while members disagreed with outsiders about the standing of their own organization, they tended to agree with them about the prestige of all other organizations in the same set. There may be something of a sociological parable in this array of findings. In these matters, at least, the judgments of Insiders are best trusted when they assess groups other than their own; that is, when Insiders judge as Outsiders.

But findings of this sort do not testify, of course, that ethnocentrism and its frequent spiritual correlate, xenophobia, fear and hatred of the alien, are incorrigible. They do, however, remind us of the widespread tendency to glorify the in-group. And this finds fullest expression when groups are subject to the stress of acute conflict. Under the stress of war, for example, even scientists imbued with the values and norms of universalism have abandoned these in favor of national loyalty. Thus, at the outset of World War I, almost a hundred German scholars and scientists — including many of the first rank, such as Brentano, Ehrlich, Haber, Eduard Meyer, Ostwald, Planck and Schmoller — could bring themselves to issue a manifesto that impugned the contributions of the enemy to science, charging nationalistic bias, logrolling, intellectual dishonesty and, when you came right down to it, the absence of creative capacity.[8]

Ethnocentrism, then, is not a constant. It becomes more intense under conditions of social conflict as under changing conditions of effective exploitation and socially induced wants for collective self-esteem. When a nation, race or ethnic group has long extolled its own merits and depreciated the qualities of others, it invites a counter-ethnocentrism. And when a once largely powerless minority acquires a socially validated sense of growing power, its members experience an intensified need for self-affirmation. Collective self-glorification, found in some measure among all groups, becomes a frequent counter-response to longstanding belittlement from without.[9]

So it is, in this country, that the centuries-long institutionalized premise that "white (and presumably only white) is true and good and beautiful" leads, under conditions of revolutionary change, to the counter-premise that "black (and presumably only black) is true and good and beautiful." And just as the social system has tacitly affirmed that in cases of conflict between whites and blacks, the whites are presumptively right, so there now develops the counter-view, finding easy confirmation in the long history of injustice visited upon American Negroes, that in cases of such conflict today, the blacks are presumptively right.

What is being proposed here is that the epistemological and ontological claims of the Insider to privileged access to social truth develops under particular social and historical conditions. Social groups or strata on the way up develop a revolutionary elan. The new thrust to control over their social and political environment finds various expressions, among them claims to special access to knowledge about their own history, psychology and culture. Understandably, this thrust does not lay claim to a black physics, chemistry, biology, or technology. For the new will to control their fate deals with the social environment, not the natural one.

Polarization in the underlying social structure becomes reflected in the polarization of claims in the intellectual and ideological domain, as groups seek to determine what

Heidegger calls the "public interpretation of reality."[10] With varying degrees of intent, groups in conflict want to make their interpretation of how things are and were and will be become the prevailing interpretation. The critical test occurs when the interpretation moves beyond the boundaries of the in-group, to be accepted by outsiders. At the extreme, it gives rise through identifiable processes of reference group behavior to the familiar case of the converted outsider validating himself by becoming overly-zealous in adhering to the doctrine of the group with which he wants to identify himself, if only symbolically.[11] He then becomes more royalist than the king, more papist than the pope. Some white social scientists, for example, understandably guilt-ridden over centuries of white racism, are prepared to outdo the group they would symbolically join. They are ready even to surrender their hardwon expert knowledge if it should run counter to the Insider doctrine. This response is perhaps epitomized in a recently televised educational program. The white curator of African ethnology at a major museum is engaged in discussion with a militant black who, as it happens, has had no prolonged ethnological training. All the same, at a crucial juncture in the discussion, the distinguished ethnologist can be heard to say: "I realize, of course, that I cannot begin to understand the black experience, in Africa or America, as you can. Won't you tell our audience about it?" Here, indeed, the Insider doctrine becomes the public interpretation.

The social process underlying the emergence of that doctrine is reasonably clear. The dominant social institutions in this country have long treated the racial identity of individuals as relevant and salient to all manner of situations in every sphere of life. For generations, neither blacks nor white, though with notably differing consequences, were permitted to forget their race. This treatment of racial identity as relevant when it is in fact functionally irrelevant to a situation is, after all, at the very core of racial discrimination. As this once firmly rooted system of discriminatory institutions and prejudicial ideology loses its hold, it leads increasingly many to become racially color-blind. But as

Tocqueville observed long ago, small and lazy social changes serve to prepare the ground for substantial and rapid change. What the Insider doctrine of the most militant blacks proposes in effect, on the level of social structure, is to take over the primacy of racial identity in every sort of situation, so long imposed upon the American Negro, and to make it a total commitment issuing from within the group rather than being imposed from without. Just as conditions of war between nations have long invited a strain toward hyper-patriotism among some national ethnocentrics, so the current conflict produces a strain toward hyper-loyalty among some racial ethnocentrics. Total commitment involves the doctrine, not merely of "our group, right or wrong," but of "our group, always right, never wrong." And the call to total commitment means of course that the one group loyalty is to be paramount, overriding all other loyalties.

This socially induced pressure toward a single, over-arching group loyalty results in a monolithic doctrine. Yet this has a way of colliding with a basic fact of social structure. Neither the Negro population nor the white consist of an undifferentiated mass. Ideology notwithstanding, both are highly differentiated — by occupation and class and politics and religion and culture. Since we all occupy various statuses and have various group affiliations of significance to us, this structural fact counters efforts to introduce the exclusive primacy of any one affiliation especially where it is function-ally irrelevant. Each significant affiliation exacts its own loyalty to values and standards and norms governing its own domain, whether religion, science or economy. But the monopolistic doctrine of the Insider calls for total ideological loyalty, in which efforts to achieve scholarly detachment and objectivity become redefined as renegadism just as ideological reinforcement of collective self-esteem becomes redefined as the higher objectivity. It is here that Negro scholars who retain their double loyalty — to the race and to the company of scholars — part company with the all-encompassing loyalty demanded by black militants. The Negro political scientist, Martin Kilson, for example, repudiates the doctrine of the Insider in just these terms:

I am opposed to proposals to make Afro-American studies into a platform for a particular ideological group, and to restrict these studies to Negro students and teachers. For, and we must be frank about this, what this amounts to is racism in reverse — black racism. I am certainly convinced that it is important for the Negro to know of his past — of his ancestors, of their strengths and weaknesses — and they should respect his knowledge, when it warrants respect, and they should question it and criticize it, when it deserves criticism. But it is of no advantage to a mature and critical understanding or appreciation of one's heritage if you approach that heritage with the assumption that it is intrinsically good or noble, and intrinsically superior to the heritage of other peoples. This is, after all, what white racists have done; and none of my militant friends in the black studies movement have convinced me that racist thought is any less vulgar and degenerate because it is used by black men.[12]

This expresses a principled rejection of the Insider doctrine as it conflicts with the canons of scholarship which transcend other group affiliations, whether national, racial or religious. As it turns out, moreover, what Insiders profess as Insiders, they themselves reject as Outsiders. When black militants engage in analysis of the so-called white society, trying to assay its power structure or to detect its vulnerabilities, they deny in practice what they affirm in doctrine. Their own behavior testifies to the tacit conviction that it is possible for even self-styled Outsiders to diagnose and to understand what they describe as an alien social structure and culture. The contrary-to-doctrine practice hints at the ideological rather than the cognitive character of the Insider-doctrine.

In formulating its mandate for parochialism, the Insider doctrine runs counter, of course, to a long history of thought. From the time of Francis Bacon, to reach no further back, students of the intellectual life have emphasized the corrupting influence of group loyalties upon the human understanding. Among Bacon's four Idols (or sources of false opinion), we need only recall the second, the Idol of the Cave. Drawing upon Plato's allegory of the cave in the *Republic*, Bacon tells how the immediate social world in which we live limits what we are prepared to perceive and how we perceive it. Dominated by the customs of our group, we maintain received opinions, distort our perceptions to see only that which accord with these opinions, and are thus led into error and ignorance which we mistake for the truth. Only when we escape from the cave and extend our vision do we provide for access to authentic knowledge. By implication, it is through the iconoclasm that comes with multiple group affiliations that we can destroy the idol of the cave and enlarge our prospects for reaching the truth. For Bacon, the dedicated Insider is peculiarly subject to the myopia of the cave.

The founding fathers of sociology in effect argued against the doctrine of the Insider without turning to the equal and opposite error of advocating the doctrine of the Outsider. In his memorable phrase, Max Weber maintained that "one need not be Caesar in order to understand Caesar."[13] In developing this, he rejects the extreme Insider doctrine which asserts that one *must* be Caesar in order to understand him just as he rejects the extreme Outsider doctrine that one must *not* be Caesar in order to understand him. Georg Simmel went on to note the distinctive roles of that incarnation of the outsider, the stranger who moves on. Not caught up in commitments to the group that work to distort perception, understanding and evaluation, the stranger can acquire the strategic role of the relatively objective inquirer. "He is freer, practically and theoretically," writes Simmel, "he surveys conditions with less prejudice; his criteria for them are more general and more objective ideals; he is not tied down in his action by habit, piety and precedent."[14] It is the stranger, too, who finds the seemingly familiar significantly unfamiliar and so is prompted to raise questions for inquiry less apt to be raised at all by insiders.

Weber and Simmel were not addressing themselves to the Insider doctrine although their observations bear upon it. That doctrine, reemerging as it has under conditions of social conflict which give it added point, has implications that reach beyond its emphasized contemporaneous scope. The Insider argues that the authentic understanding of groups, *here and now*, can be attained only by those who are directly engaged in the life of these groups. But taken seriously, the doctrine implies far more. It puts in question the validity of just about all historical writing. For if direct engagement in the life of groups is essential to understanding them, the only authentic history is contemporary history, written presumably by those most fully involved in making it. Rather than constituting only the raw materials of history, the documents prepared by engaged Insiders become all there is to history. But once he elected to write the history of a time other than his own, even the most dedicated Insider, of the racial, ethnic, national or religious variety, would inevitably become the Outsider, condemned to everlasting error and misunderstanding. On this view, all historians examining the past join most social scientists examining past or present as Outsiders beyond the pale.

Writing some twenty years ago in quite another connection, Claude Levi-Strauss noted the parallelism between history and ethnography. Both subjects, he observes, "are concerned with societies *other* than the one in which we live. Whether this *otherness* is due to remoteness in time (however slight) or to remoteness in space, or even to cultural heterogeneity, is of secondary importance compared to the basic similarity of perspective."[15]

As we have seen, the Insider doctrine conceives of groups as monolithic, ignoring their internal differentiation which should in turn make for multiple insider and outsider perspectives. It is of particular interest, then, that Levi-Strauss goes on at once to consider the implications of this structural fact, as he asks about the goals of the two disciplines of history and ethnography:

Is it the exact reconstruction of what has happended, or is it happening, in the society under study? To assert this would be to forget that in both cases we are dealing with systems of representations which differ for each member of the group and which, on the whole, differ from the representations of the investigator. The best ethnographic study will never make the reader a native. The French Revolution of 1789 as lived through by an aristocrat is not the same phenomenon as the Revolution of 1789 lived through by a *sans-culotte*, and neither would correspond to the Revolution of 1789 as conceived by Michelet or Taine. All that the historian or ethnographer can do, and all that we can expect of either of them, is to enlarge a specific experience to the dimensions of a more general one, which thereby becomes accessible *as experience* to men of another country or another epoch. And in order to succeed, both historian and ethnographer must have the same qualities: skill, precision, a sympathetic approach, and objectivity.

The quartet of qualities required by the ethnographer and historian are not peculiar to either insider or outsider. Yet, as Simmel has suggested and as experience seems to confirm, in matters historical and sociological the prospects for achieving objectivity and special insights may actually be somewhat better for the outsider. That, at least, seems to have been involved in one of the most perceptive accounts of American society. Soon after it appeared in 1835, Tocqueville's *Democracy in America* was acclaimed as a masterly work by "an accomplished foreigner." Tocqueville himself observed that "there are certain truths which Americans can only learn from strangers." As is well known, these included what he described as the tyranny of majority opinion and the particular system of stratification which even in that time involved a widespread preoccupation with relative status in the community that left "Americans so restless in the midst of their prosperity."[16] (This *is* Tocqueville, not Galbraith, writing.)

What was in the case of Tocqueville an unplanned circumstance became, just a century later, a matter of deliberate decision. Casting about for a scholar who might make a thoroughgoing critical study of the Negro in America, the Carnegie Corporation searched for an outsider, preferably one, as they put it, drawn from a country "of high intellectual and scholarly standards but with no background or traditions of imperialism." These twin conditions of course swiftly narrowed the scope of the search. Switzerland and the Scandanavian countries alone seemed to qualify, with the quest ending, as we know, with the selection of Gunnar Myrdal. In the preface to *An American Dilemma*, Myrdal reflected on his status as an outsider who, in his words, "had never been subject to the strains involved in living in a black-white society" and who, as "a stranger to the problem . . . has had perhaps a greater awareness of the extent to which human valuations everywhere enter into our scientific discussion

of the Negro problem."[17] The importance of the detachment
from entangling loyalties that come with being an outsider
was repeatedly noted in reviews of the book. J. S. Redding,
for one, observed that "as a European, Myrdal has no American sensibilities to protect. He hits hard with fact and
interpretation."[18] For another, Robert S. Lynd saw as a
prime merit of this outsider that he was free to find out for
himself "without any side glances as to what was politically
expedient."[19] And for a third, Frank Tannebaum noted that
Myrdal brought "objectivity in regard to the special foibles
and shortcomings in American life. As an outsider, he showed
the kind of objectivity which would seem impossible for one
reared within the American scene."[20]

In the judgment of these critical minds, then, the Outsider,
far from being excluded from an objective understanding
of an alien society, could bring needed perspectives to it.
I note only in passing that other spheres of experience have
found distinctive roles for the insider and the outsider. In
the domain of technology, for example, it was suggested a
generation ago that the "cardinal inventions are due to men
outside the occupation affected, and the minor, perfective
investions to insiders."[21] And in a recent and far more
exacting inquiry, Joseph Ben-David found that the pro-
fessionalization of scientific research "does not in itself
decrease the chances of innovation by outsiders" to the
differentiated fields of science.[22]

Consider also that a variety of institutional arrangements
are based on the premise that the drawing in of outsiders
will make for detachment and equity. The institution of the
arbitrator, for one example, involves a judicial process in
which one or more outsiders to a conflict make a binding
decision based on the merits of the dispute.

The cumulative point of this variety of cases is not, of
course, the proposal to replace the extreme Insider doctrine
by an extreme and equally vulnerable Outsider doctrine. It is,
rather, to transform the original issue altogether. We no
longer ask whether it is the Insider or the Outsider who has
privileged or monopolistic access to social truth; instead, we
consider their distinctive and interactive roles in the process

of truth-seeking.

The intellectual interchange between insiders and outsiders is often obscured by the rhetoric that commonly attends group conflict. If we listen only to that rhetoric, we are easily misled. Almost we are brought to believe that there really is something like antithetical "black knowledge" and "white knowledge," that there is a chaos of conflicting assertions about society with no basis for adjudicating rival claims. Yet the boundaries between insiders and outsiders tend to be far more permeable than this allows. Just as with the process of competition generally, so with the competition of ideas. Competing or conflicting groups take over ideas and concepts developed by the other side. Even in the course of social polarization, conceptions with cognitive value are utilized all apart from their source. Concepts of power structure, the dysfunctions of established institutions, co-optation and findings associated with these concepts have been put forward by social scientists who happen to be white. Yet they are not exactly ignored by self-described black Insiders. Nathan Hare, one of the more articulate exponents of the black Insider doctrine, for example, makes use of the notion of the self-fulfilling prophecy in trying to explain how it is, in this day and age, that organizations run by blacks find it had to get along. As he puts it, "White people thought that we could not have any institutions which were basically black which were of good quality. This has the effect of self-fulfilling prophecy, because if you think that black persons cannot possibly have a good bank, you don't put your money in it . . . The blacks even do the same thing. And this makes your prediction, which wasn't true in the beginning, come out to be true."[23]

Such diffusion of ideas across the proclaimed boundaries of groups has long been noted. In one of his more astute analyses, Karl Mannheim states the general case for the emergence of knowledge that transcends even profound conflicts between groups:

Syntheses [he observes] owe their existence to the same social process that brings about polarization; groups take over the modes of thought and intellectual achievements of their adversaries under the simple law of 'competition on the basis of achievement.' . . . in the socially-differentiated thought process, even the opponent is ultimately forced to adopt those categories and forms of thought which are most appropriate in a given type of world order. In the economic sphere, one of the possible results of competition is that one competitor is compelled to catch up with the other's techno-logical advances. In just the same way, whenever groups compete for having their interpretation of reality accepted as the correct one, it may happen that one of the groups takes over from the adversary some fruitful hypothesis or category — anything that promises cognitive gain . . . [In due course, it becomes possible] to find a position from which both kinds of thought can be envisaged in their partial correctness, yet at the same time also interpreted as sub-ordinate aspects of a higher synthesis.[24]

The essential point is that, with or without intent, the process of intellectual exchange takes place precisely because the conflicting groups are in interaction. The extreme black Insider doctrine, for example, affects the thinking of socio-logists who reject its extravagant claims. Intellectual conflict sensitizes them to aspects of their subject which they have otherwise not taken into account.

As a case in point of this process of intellectual sensitiza-tion through conflict, I take what might be described as the composite pattern of social sadism and sociological euphem-ism. We can think of social sadism as something more than a mere metaphor. By the term, I refer to social structures which are so organized as to inflict systematically pain, humiliation, suffering and deep frustration upon social groups and strata in those structures. This need have little or nothing to do with psychic propensities of individuals to take delight in cruelty. It is an objective, socially organized set of situations which have these cruel consequences, what-ever their diverse historical sources and whatever the social processes which maintain them.

This type of sadistic social structure is often linked up with a distinctive sociological perspective on that structure which can be described as the perspective of the sociological euphemism. By this, I do not mean explicit ideological support of the structure couched in sociological terms.

Rather, I mean a conceptual apparatus that conceals or at least systematically ignores intense human experience of pain, suffering, humiliation, and so on. Such analytically useful concepts as reward-system, social stratification, out-groups, social exchange, etc. tend to be altogether bland in the fairly precise sense of being unperturbing, suave and soothing in effect. But be it noted, the impersonal concepts, analytically useful, as they are, also manage to exclude from systematic attention the intense feelings of pain, suffering and humilation which are the experience of people caught up in these social patterns. The concepts screen out this profondly personal experience and, in this sense, they become sociological euphemisms.

Nor is there an easy solution to the problem of the sociological euphemism. True, we have all been warned off the Whiteheadian fallacy of misplaced concreteness, the fallacy of assuming that the particular concepts we employ to examine the flow of events capture their entire content. No more than in other fields of inquiry are sociological concepts designed to reproduce the concrete entirety of the psychosocial reality to which they refer. So much for the methodological rationale of conceptual abstraction.

But now consider empirical outcomes of this established practice of employing bland sociological concepts which inevitably abstract from the concreteness of social life. Often, it is only a short step from this practice to the tacit assumption that the aspects of reality which these concepts help us understand *are the only aspects worth trying to understand*. There is a special kind of irony involved here. The more intellectually powerful a set of sociological conceptions has proved to be, the less the incentive to elaborate it in ways designed to catch up the humanly significant aspects of the psychological reality which it neglects. As I have said, the social scientist, at first aware that he is abstracting from the reality in order to deal systematically only with selected aspects of it, comes in due course to act as though these have been shown to be the only aspects worth considering. The ground is prepared for the next seemingly small but altogether conclusive step. The social scientist comes to act as though aspects of the reality which are neglected by his analytical apparatus *do not exist at all.* In this way, even the most conscientious social scientist is often led to convert his scientific concepts and models into scientific euphemisms.

It is this tendency toward the soiological euphemism, I suggest, that is now being forced upon the attention of (primarily but not exclusively white) social scientists who inquire into the structure of race relations. No one has put this more forcefully and succinctly than Kenneth Clark:

> . . . more privileged individuals may understandably need to shield themselves from the inevitable conflict and pain which would result from acceptance of the fact that they *are* accessories to profound injustice. The tendency to discuss disturbing social issues such as racial discrimination, segregation, and economic exploitation in detached, legal, political, socio-economic, or psychological terms as if these persistent problems did not involve the suffering of actual human beings is so contrary to empirical evidence that it must be interpreted as a protective device.[25]

Perhaps I have said enough to exemplify the point that Insider and Outsider perspectives can converge through the reciprocal borrowing of ideas and the developing of complementary and overlapping foci of attention in the formulation of problems. But such potentials for synthesis are not often realized on their own. Increased social polarization stand in the way. For as balance theory in psychology[26] indicates and as the study of mass communications behavior finds,[27] under conditions of acute conflict, each hostile camp develops selective perceptions of what is going on in the other. Perspectives and opinions become self-confirming as both Insiders and Outsiders tend to shut themselves off from ideas and information at odds with their own views. They see in the other primarily what their hostile dispositions alert them to see and then promptly mistake the part for the whole. In the process, each group becomes less and less motivated to examine the ideas of the other, since there is manifestly small point in doing so. The members of each group scan the out-group's writings just enough to find ammunition for new fusillades.[28]

This process of selective attention to ideas of the other makes for the clash of all-or-none doctrines. Even intellectual orientations which are not substantively contradictory come to be regarded as though they are. Either the Insider *or* the Outsider has access to the sociological truth. In the midst of polarized social conflict, there is little room for the third, uncommitted party who tries to convert that conflict into intellectual criticism. Typically, these would be non-combatants are caught in the crossfire between hostile camps. Depending on the partisan vocabulary of abuse which happens to prevail, they are tagged as intellectual mugwumps, pharisees or renegades, or somewhat more generously, as "mere eclectics" with the epithet, by convention, making it unnecessary to examine the substance of what is being asserted or how far it holds true. Perhaps worst of all, they are defined as mere middle-of-the-roaders who, through timidity or expediency, will not see that they try to escape the fundamental conflict between unalloyed sociological good and unalloyed sociological evil.

Through the transition from social conflict to intellectual criticism there can develop trade-offs between the distinctive strengths and weaknesses of Insider and Outsider perspectives of a kind which can enlarge the chances for the sound and relevant interpretation of human societies. For much of the argument depends on what is meant by "understanding," whether sympathetic, insightful or whatever. The introspective meanings of experience within the group probably have a better prospect of being reconstructed by those who have themselves had that experience. But understanding includes much beyond this. It includes an empirically confirmable sense of the conditions and often complex processes in which people are caught up without much awareness of what is going on. To analyze and understand these requires a theoretical and technical apparatus which has, as such, nothing to do with one's status as Insider or Outsider. Beyond that, it requires enough detachment and trained capacity to assay evidence on its merits and without regard for what the analysis implies for the worth of one's own group. And here, the Outsider may even have the edge.

Apart from all this, there is a fundamental reason for the irrelevance of Insider and Outsider identities to the value and validity of the intellectual product. For its is the character of an intellectual *discipline* that its rules of the game have been adopted before they are used in analyzing a given problem. Good intellectual work and bad may turn up to different extent among Insiders and Outsiders as an artifact of immediate local conditions and that is itself a difficult problem for investigation. But the intellectual criteria, as distinct from the social ones, for judging that work transcend the group allegiances extraneous to it.

Criteria of craftsmanship in science and learning become increasingly universalistic, cutting across differences in the other social affiliations and loyalties of scholars and scientists. Commitments to these values of intellectual integrity, scepticism and universalism cut across and dampen the group-induced pressure to advance the interests of a particular group at the expense of these values. Historically, the institutions supporting the growth of knowledge have developed a degree of functional autonomy. It is that autonomy which still enables the pursuit of truth to transcend other loyalties, as Michael Polanyi, more than the rest of us, has long recognized. "A man who has learned to respect the truth," he writes, "will feel entitled to uphold the truth against the very society which has taught him to respect it. He will indeed demand respect for himself on the grounds of his own respect for the truth, and this will be accepted, even against their own inclinations, by those who share his basic convictions. Such is the equality of men in a free society."[29]

An occasion such as this one celebrating an episode in the intellectual domain clearly calls for a peroration. Here, then, is mine. Insiders and Outsiders, unite. You have nothing to lose but your claims. You have a world of understanding to win.

Endnotes

1.   The general idea of the conditions making for intensified pro-
     blems in the sociology of knowledge is summarized in my 1945
     paper on the sociology of knowledge, reprinted in R. K. Merton:
     Social Theory and Social Structure. New York: The Free Press,
     1968, esp. at pp. 510-514.

2.   Ernst Krieck: *Nationalpolitische Erziehung*. Leipzig: Armanen
     Verlag, 1935 (19th printing).

3.   Nathan Hare, quoted by John H. Bunzel: "Black Studies at San
     Francisco State," *The Public Interest*, Fall 1968, 13, 32.

4.   On the general point of shifting boundaries between insiders and
     outsiders, see Merton, *op. cit.*, pp. 338-342, 479-480.

5.   Ralph W. Conant: "Black Power in Urban America," *Library
     Journal*, May 15, 1968, 93, pp. 1963-67.

6.   William T. Fontaine: " 'Social Determination' in the Writings of
     Negro Scholars," *American Journal of Sociology*, 1944, 49, pp.
     302-315.

7.   Theodore Caplow: *Principles of Organization*. New York: Har-
     court, Brace & World, 1964, pp. 213-216.

8.   Merton: *op. cit.*, p. 608.

9.   These observations, made some twenty years ago, are reprinted in
     ibid., p. 431.

10. M. Heidegger: "Sein und Zeit." *Jahrbuch fur Philosophie und
     Phanemonologische Forschung*, 1927, VIII as cited and discussed
     by Karl Mannheim: *Essays on the Sociology of Knowledge*. New
     York: Oxford University Press, 1952, p. 196ff.

11. For this general process of reference group orientation, see
     Merton: *op. cit.*, pp. 350, 405-6.

12. Martin Kilson: "Black Studies Movement: a Plea for Perspective,"
     Crisis, October 1969, 76, pp. 327-332, at 329.

13. Max Weber: *Gesammelte Aufsatze zur Wissenschaftslehre*,
     Tubingen: Mohr, 1922, pp. 5-7.

14. *The Sociology of Georg Simmel*, trans. and ed. by Kurt H. Wolff.
     New York: The Free Press, 1950, pp. 404-5. Simmel's observa-
     tions of course go back to the early part of the century. For some
     field work observations on the thesis that "the outsider has
     'stranger value' ", see R. K. Merton: "Selected Problems of Field
     Work in the Planned Community," *American Sociological Review*,
     1947, XII, pp. 304-312, at 305. I understand that the Australian
     anthropologist O. A. Oeser has discussed stranger-value in field
     work but I have been unable to locate the source.

15. Claude Levi-Strauss: *Structural Anthropology*. New York: Basic
     Books, 1963, p. 16. The essay from which this is drawn was first
     published in 1949.

16. Alexis de Tocqueville: *Democracy in America*. New York:

A. A. Knopf, 1945. The remarks on stranger-value are in the introduction; the famous phrase is in the title of chapter 13 in volume 2, book 2.

17. Gunnar Myrdal *et al*: *An American Dilemma*. New York: Harper & Bros., 1944, pp. xviii-xix.

18. J. S. Redding: review in *The New Republic*, March 20, 1944, 110, pp. 384-386.

19. Robert S. Lynd: "Prison for our Genius," *Saturday Review*, April 22, 1944, 27, pp. 5-7, 27.

20. Frank Tannenbaum: "An American Dilemma," *Political Science Quarterly*, Sept. 1944, 59, pp. 321-340.

21. S. C. Gilfillan: *The Sociology of Invention*. Chicago: Follett, 1935, p. 88.

22. Joseph Ben-David: "Role and Innovations in Medicine,"*American Journal of Sociology*, May 1960, LXV, pp. 557-568.

23. Nathan Hare, interview reported in *U. S. News and World Report*, 22 May 1967, 65.

24. Mannheim: *op. cit.*, pp. 221-2, 223.

25. Kenneth Clark: *Dark Ghetto*. New York: Harper & Row, 1965, p. 75.

26. I refer to the early work of Fritz Heider and its theoretical development to the present day.

27. For example, the analysis by Herbert H. Hyman and Paul B. Sheatsley: "Some reasons why information campaigns fail," *Public Opinion and Propaganda* from the *Public Opinion Quarterly*, Fall 1947, 11, pp. 412-423.

28. Drawn from R. K. Merton: "Social Conflict in styles of socio-logical work," *Transactions*, Fourth World Congress of Sociology, 1961, III, pp. 21-46. But see the recent overview of psychological evidence on self-selected exposure to supportive information by Jonathan L. Freedman and David O. Sears: "Selective exposure," In. L. Berkowtiz, ed., *Advances in Experimental Social Psychology*. New York: Academic Press, 1965, pp. 58-97. Their conclusions do not bear directly, in my judgment, on the flow of information across boundaries of groups of scholars in acute social conflict.

29. Michael Polanyi: *The Study of Man*. London: Routledge & Kegan Paul, 1959, pp. 61-62.

Meaninglessness: A Challenge to Psychiatry

Viktor E. Frankl

The title that has been given to this presentation, reads, "Meaninglessness: A Challenge to Psychiatry." Really, however, it should read, "The Feeling of Meaninglessness: A Challenge to Psychiatry." In fact, a psychiatrist today is confronted more than ever before with patients — or shouldn't I rather say nonpatients? — who are complaining of a sense of futility. Let me just quote from a letter I recently received from a young American student: "I am a 22 year old with degree, car, security and the availability of more sex and power than I need. Now I have only to explain to myself what it all means." However, such people are complaining not only of a feeling of meaninglessness but also of a sense of emptiness and that is why I have described this condition in terms of the "existential vacuum."[1]

There is no doubt that the existential vacuum is increasing and spreading. According to a report I have recently been shown, 2 years ago the percentage of those suffering from it, among a population of 500 Viennese youngsters, has increased, within the last 2 years, from 30% to 80%.[2] And even in Africa the existential vacuum is spreading, particularly among the academic youth.[3] Also Freudians are fully aware of the occurrence and presence of this phenomenon, and so are Marxists. At an international meeting of psychoanalysts it has been stated that ever more patients are suffering from a lack of life content, rather than clinical symptomatology, and that this state of affairs may well account for so-called interminable analyses because, as the

71

Freudians have contended, in such cases the psychoanalytic treatment has become the only life content available to the patient. And as to the Marxists, only recently the Head of the Department of Psychotherapy at Karl Marx University in Leipzig has confessed to the frequency of the existential vacuum as evidenced by her own investigations. As the Head of the Department of Psychiatry at a Czech university puts it, the existential vacuum is passing the borders between capitalist and communist countries "without a visa."[4]

If you ask me for a brief explanation I would say that the existential vacuum derives from the following facts. Unlike an animal, man is no longer told by drives and instincts what he must do. And in contract to man in former times, he is no longer told by traditions and values what he should do. Now neither knowing what he must do nor what he should do he sometimes does not even know what he basically wishes to do. Instead, he wishes to do what other people do — which is conformism — or he does what other people wish him to do — which is totalitarianism.

In addition to these two effects of the existential vacuum there is a third one, namely, neuroticism. Per se the existential vacuum is no neurosis, at least it is not a neurosis in the strictly clinical sense. If it is a neurosis at all it would have to be diagnosed as a sociogenic neurosis. However, there are also cases in which the existential vacuum eventuates in clinical symptomatology. Such patients are suffering from what I have called "noogenic neuroses." It goes to the credit of James C. Crumbaugh to have developed a special test diagnostically to differentiate the noogenic from other forms of neurosis.[5,6] Elisabeth St. Lukas,[7] although using a different test, has arrived at the same percentage of noogenic neuroses as Crumbaugh, namely, 20%.

As to the existential vacuum, however, which in itself is not a neurosis, a statistical survey recently showed that among my European students 25% knew this "abyss experience," as it may be called in counterdistinction to the "peak experience," from their own experience. Among my American students it was not 25 but 60%.

A communist psychiatrist found out that among various

populations of Czech students the degree of the existential vacuum as measured by Crumbaugh's test was even higher than the degree observed and reported among students in the USA. A year later, however, it turned out that the figure had become markedly lower. In the meantime, most of the students had become involved in Dubcek's movement, his battle for political liberalization and for the humanization of communism. They had been given a cause for which to fight, for which to live and, unfortunately, also to die. I wonder what the percentage of the existential vacuum among the Czech students might be today.

On the average, however, the fact remains that in America the existential vacuum makes itself more noticeable than in Europe. As I see it, this is due to the exposition of the average American student to an indoctrination along the lines of reductionism. To cite an instance, there is a book in which man is defined as "nothing but a complex biochemical mechanism powered by a combustion system which energizes computors with prodigious storage facilities for retaining encoded information." Or, to quote another example, man is defined as a "naked ape." By offering our students such reductionist concepts of man their existential vacuum is reinforced. I well remember how I felt when I was a thirteen-year-old junior high school student and our natural science teacher told us that life in the final analysis was "nothing but a combustion process, an oxidation process." I sprang to my feet and said, "Professor, if this is the case, what meaning then does life have?" To be sure, in his case reductionism had taken on the form of "oxidationism."

A study by R. N. Gray and associates[8] showed that during medical school cynicism as a rule increases while humanitarianism decreases. Only after completion of medical studies this trend is reversed but unfortunately not in all subjects. Small wonder, I would say. Just consider the two definitions offered by the author in whose paper the study was quoted. Man is defined as nothing but "an adaptive control system," and values are defined as nothing but "homeostatic restraints in a stimulus-response process."[9] According to another reductionist definition of values, they are "nothing but reaction formations and defense mechanisms." Why, as for myself, I am not prepared to live for the sake of my reaction formations, even less to die for the sake of my defense mechanisms.

A famous Freudian psychoanalyst devoted two volumes to Goethe. "In the 1,538 pages," a review on the book reads, "the author portrays to us a genius with the earmarks of a manic-depressive, paranoid, and epileptoid disorder, of homosexuality, incest, voyeurism, exhibitionism, fetishism, impotence, narcissism, obsessive-compulsive neurosis, hysteria, megalomania, etc. He seems to focus almost exclusively upon the instinctual dynamic forces that underlie the artistic product. We are led to believe that Goethe's work is but the result of pregenital fixations. His struggle does not really aim for an ideal, for beauty, for values, but for the overcoming of an embarrassing problem of premature ejaculation."[10] How wise and cautious was Freud, as compared with his epigones, when he once remarked that sometimes a cigar may be a cigar and nothing but a cigar. To be sure, if I were a Freudian myself, I would have to interpret this statement as a rationalization of his own cigar smoking.

The reductionist interpretation of values is likely to undermine and erode the enthusiasm of youth. As example, let me report the following observation. A young American couple returned from Africa where they had served as Peace Corps volunteers, completely fed up and disgusted. At the outset, they had to participate in mandatory group sessions led by a psychologist who played a game somewhat as follows: "Why did you join the Peace Corps?" "We wanted to help people less privileged." "So you must be superior to them." "In a way." "So there must be in you, in your unconscious, a need to prove to yourself that you are superior." "Well, we never thought of it that way but you are a psychologist, you certainly know better." And so it went on. They were indoctrinated in interpreting their idealism and altruism as hang-ups. Even worse, they "were constantly on each other's backs, playing the 'what's *your* hidden motive' game," according to their report.

Unmasking is perfectly legitimate but it must stop as soon

as one is confronted with what is genuine, genuinely human, in man. If it does not, the only thing that is unmasked is the unmasking psychologist's own "hidden motive," namely, his unconscious need to debase and depreciate the humanness of man. What then starts is "hyper-interpretation," as I would call it, and it proves to be most dangerous when it comes to self-interpretation. We psychiatrists have met many patients who are suffering from, and crippled by, the obsessive compulsion to analyze themselves, to observe and watch themselves, to reflect upon themselves. The cultural climate that is predominant and prevalent in the U.S., makes for the danger that this compulsion becomes a collective obsessive neurosis. Just consider a recent study by Edith Weisskopf-Joelson and associates.[11] It shows that the value that ranks highest among American college students, is self-interpretation. I see in these findings another indication of the existential vacuum. As the boomerang returns to the hunter who has thrown it, only in case that it has missed its target, the prey, man returns to himself, reflects upon himself and beomes overly concerned with self-interpretation only in case that he has missed his mission, as it were, having been frustrated in his search for meaning. The Freudians' experience with patients in whom, due to the lack of life content, the psychoanalytic treatment has become a substitute, comes to mind.

According to Edith Weisskopf-Joelson and associates, the value that ranks highest next to self-interpretation is self-actualization. However, my contention is that ultimately man can actualize himself only by fulfilling a meaning out there in the world rather than within himself. In other words, self-actualization is an effect of what I call "self-transcendence."[12] By this I mean the fact that being human means relating, and being directed, to something, or someone, other than oneself, be it a meaning to fulfill, or another being to encounter. Pindar's imperative that one should become what he is, that is to say, man should actualize his potentialities, is tenable provided that we rush and hurry to add Karl Jaspers' words "what one is, he has become through that cause which he has made his own." Or, as Abraham H. Maslow[13] puts it, the "business of self-actualization" can best be carried out "via a commitment to an important job."

One of the two aspects of self-transcendence, namely, reaching out for a meaning to fulfill, is identical with what I call the "will to meaning." This concept has been empirically corroborated by James C. Crumbaugh and Leonard T. Maholick.[14] Rolf H. Von Eckartsberg of Duquesne University's Department of Psychology also thinks that "a basic 'will to meaning' has to be assumed as an important motive-value," and that, in fact, "individuals aspire toward the fulfillment of values, the achievement of a meaningful life".[15] Abraham H. Maslow bluntly declares: "I agree entirely with Frankl that man's primary concern is his will to meaning".[16] Even behind the Iron Curtain research conducted by S. Kratochvil and I. Planova of the Department of Psychology of the University of Brno (Czechoslovakia) has offered evidence "that the will to meaning is really a specific need not reducible ₁to other needs, and is in greater or smaller degree present in all human beings. The relevance of the frustration of this need," the authors continue to contend, "was documented also by case material, concering neurotic and depressive patients. In some cases the existential vacuum had a relevant role as an etiological factor in the origin of the neurosis or of the suicidal attempt."[17] It should be noted that these findings have been obtained by tests and statistics. The same holds of data that have been gathered by Elisabeth S. Lukas.[7] They concern 1,340 subjects. After being computerized the data have validated the concepts of a will to meaning in terms of the original and primary motivation operant in man.

A recent study by James C. Crumbaugh, Sister Mary Raphael and Raymond R. Shrader employs a test designed to measure the will to meaning. The highest scores were obtained among well motivated professional and successful business populations. This supports Theodor A. Kotchen's hypothesis[18] that the will to meaning is a reliable criterion of mental health. Conversely, lack of meaning and purpose is indicative of emotional maladjustment; for example, eighteen out of twenty alcoholics looked upon their existence as meaningless and without purpose, as Annemarie Von Forstmeyer[19] has shown in a dissertation presented to the United States International University.

It is the frustration of the will to meaning that brings about the will to power as well as the "will to pleasure,"[20] i.e., the pleasure principle. The latter is the pivot on which the motivation theory of Freudian psychoanalysis hinges. Adlerian psychology, in turn, ascribes an important role in the etiology of neuroses to the striving for superiority which, after all, is an expression of the will to power. Since Freud and Adler had to deal with neurotic patients, that is to say, with people frustrated in their will to meaning, it is understandable that they thought that man is basically concerned with pleasure or power, respectively, rather than meaning.

Our own hypothesis that the will to pleasure is a substitute for the frustrated will to meaning, has been corroborated and validated by statistical research. People visiting Vienna's Prater, a place that is somewhat comparable to New York's Coney Island, proved to be more existentially frustrated than the average population of Vienna.[7] Incidentally, the average population of various cities proved to be existentially frustrated to the same degree.[21]

The will to pleasure not only contradicts the self-transcendent quality of the human reality but also defeats itself. It is the very pursuit of happiness what thwarts happiness. Happiness cannot be pursued. It must ensue. This is due to the fact that happiness is availalbe only as a by-product namely, the side effect of living out the self-transcendence of existence. Once that one has fulfilled a meaning, or is loving another human being, happiness occurs by itself. On the other hand, the more one makes happiness an aim, the more he misses the aim. This is most conspicuous in cases of sexual neurosis such as frigidity or impotence. Sexual performance or experience are strangled to the extent to which they are made either an object of attention or an objective of intention. I have called the first "hyper-reflection," and the second "hyper-intention." But both phenomena are observable also on a mass level. The trend to hyper-interpretation as it is pervasive in the U. S. may be conceived of in terms of a collective hyper-reflection. With regard to a collective hyper-intention, just consider the emphasis that public opinion places on sexual achievement. This emphasis spawns preoccupations and apprehensions. People are overly concerned with sexual success, and ridden with the fear of sexual failure. But fear tends to make come true precisely that which one is afraid of. Thus a vicious circle is established. It accounts for much of the case load regarding sexual neuroses which today confronts a psychiatrist.

On a mass level the existential vacuum invites sexual libido to hypertrophy. The result is an inflation of sex. Like the inflation on the money market it is associated with a devaluation. More specifically, sex is devaluated insofar as it is dehumanized. Because human sex is always more than mere sex — it serves as the bodily expression of a relation on the human level, it functions as a vehicle of a personal relationship. In other words, human sex is an incarnation of love. "The people who can't love," says Maslow,[22] "don't get the same kind of thrill out of sex as the people who can love." That is to say, if for no other reason we would have to recommend for the sake of pleasure that sex is rehumanized. For rehumanized sex is more rewarding than dehumanized sex even in terms of "thrill."

Only recently this recommendation was substantiated by a report on 20,000 responses to 101 questions about sexual attitudes and practices. It turned out that among the factors contributing to high orgasm and potency rates "the most important" one was "romanticism."[23]

It goes without saying that the sexual instinct cannot in itself be human. After all, it is not only a property of human being but animals share it with them. Rather would it be appropriate and adequate to say that in man the sexual instinct is more or less humanized, as the case may be. As a matter of fact, in him the sexual maturation is characterized by three developmental stages in the course of which the sexual instinct approaches and approximates the potential of human sex, that is, its becoming an embodiment of love, only successively.

In characterizing the individual stages we start with

Freud's differentation between the goal of an instinct and the instinct's object. At the immature level only a goal is sought and the goal is tension reduction irrespective of the way in which it is attained. Masturbation may do. According to Freud the mature stage is reached when the sexual instinct centers and focuses on the normal sexual intercourse. This presupposes an object. The object, however, is not enough to guarantee a mature sexual life. As long as an individual "uses a partner simply for the purpose of reducing sexual tension," he really "masturbates on the partner."[23] But as I see it, to the individual who is mature, the partner is in no way a means to an end. Rather what takes place, is an encounter which is a partnership on the human level, and it takes place on the human level only when the humanness of the partner is recognized — even more, his uniqueness. And getting hold of his uniqueness means loving him.

Unless I see in the object a subject, a person, unless I humanize and personalize the partnership, I wind up with promiscuity. As masturbation means being contented with tension reduction — likewise promiscuity means stopping short of taking a step beyond, both, goal and object. On the other hand, as long as I remain at the mere goal level my sexual instinct is catered by pornography, and as long as I stay at the mere object level, my sexual instinct is catered by prostitutes.

Promiscuity and pornography are the marks of fixation, or regression, to immature levels of development. It is not wise publicly to glorify, the indulgence in such patterns of regressive behavior by confusing it with progressive mentality. As to pornography, freedom from censorship is invoked when freedom to make money is meant. As compared with the hypocrisy of businessmen working in the field of sex education, I praise the honesty of the call girls who bluntly confess that they are only out to make money by sex. And as to promiscuity, it contradicts the humanness of man on biological as well as psychological grounds. As the ethologist Irenaeus Eibl-Eibesfeldt recently pointed out, in man's biological ancestors sexual behavior has also a social function to carry out — a fact that makes for monogamous types of behavior in primates. At the psychological level promiscuity is promulgated together with intimacy. The latter is believed even to be the answer to the ills of our age. However, I think that what is needed in this age of population explosion is existential privacy rather than sexual intimacy.

Speaking of population explosion I would like to touch on the Pill. It is not only counteracting the population explosion but, as I see it, its main service goes beyond birth-control. Thanks to the Pill it is possible not only in theory but also in practice to recognize that it is love what makes sex human: this is possible because the Pill makes sex independent of procreation. Only now sex is free from being a means to an end, be it that the end is dictated by the pleasure principle or the procreation instinct. After this emancipation in two dimensions sex acquires the status of a human phenomenon.

After discussing the diagnostic aspect of the issue at hand, the feeling of meaninglessness, let us take up its therapeutic aspect by asking the question what we may do about it — we psychiatrists. It cannot be enough to do what recently was reported to me by a letter I received from a reader who wrote to me: "I have had recurrent depressive states until two days ago a psychiatrist at Harvard University (where I am a student) told me bluntly that 'your life is meaningless, you have nothing to look forward to, I am surprised that you haven't committed suicide.' " Is that all a psychiatrist has to offer? I do not think so. But are not traditions and values crumbling? How then are we to offer meaning and purpose to our patients? This is possible on the grounds of the fact that what is transmitted by traditions and consequently affected by their decay is only values but not meanings.[24] Meanings are not transmitted by traditions because, in contrast to values which are universal, meanings are unique. They refer to unique situations — and equally unique persons confronting them.

It goes to the credit of Crumbaugh and Maholick[14] to have shown that the discovery of meaning has something to do with a Gestalt perception. By the same token, meanings prove to be objective rather than merely subjective. Max Wertheimer, the founder of Gestalt psychology, also observed that "the demands" of a situation, its "requirements, are objective qualities."[25]

Certainly there are also subjective meanings — such as those that are available in that state of intoxication which is induced by LSD. Suddenly the world takes on infinite meaningfulness. And small wonder that those who are caught in the existential vacuum, resort to LSD. However, what they then provide themselves with, is mere feelings of meaningfulness. And it might well be that the "acid heads" in the long run wind up as those animals did which had been used by Olds and Milner in the course of self-stimulation experiments. They inserted electrodes into the hypothalamus of rats and whenever they closed the electric circuit the rats to all appearance experienced either sexual orgasm or the satisfaction of the ingestion of food. When the rats then learned to jump on the lever and by so doing close the electric circuit themselves they become addicted to this business and pressed the lever up to 50,000 times a day. And you know what I regard to be most remarkable? These animals then neglected the real sexual partners and the real food that had been offered to them. And I think that the "acid heads" who confine themselves to the mere feelings of meaningfulness may by-pass the true meanings which are in store, in wait for them, to be fulfilled by them out there is the world rather than within their own psyche.

Let us now ask ourselves by what man is led and guided in his search for meaning. It is my contention that this function is carried out by conscience. Conscience may be defined as a means to discover meanings, to "sniff them out," as it were. In fact, conscience lets us arrive at the unique meaning gestalts dormant in all the unique situations as they form a string called a man's life. In so far as the perception of such meaning gestalts boils down to the interpretation of a given life situation, Karl Barth was right when he said that "conscience is the true interpreter of life."

Conscience is a human phenomenon. However it is also an all too human phenomenon. It not only leads us to meaning but may as well lead us astray. This is part and parcel of the human condition. Conscience may err and I cannot know for absolutely sure whether my conscience is right and another one's conscience that tells him something different is wrong or the reverse is true. That is not to say that there is no truth. There is truth and there can be only one truth. However no one can ever know for absolutely sure whether it is he who has arrived at this truth.

In an age such as ours, in the age of meaninglessness, education, instead of confining itself to transmitting traditions and knowledge, must see its principal assignment in refining one's conscience — his only capacity still to find meanings, despite the wane of traditions and values. In other words, the crumbling of universal values can be counteracted only by finding the unique meanings. In an age in which the Ten Commandments are losing their unconditional validity in the eyes of so many people, man must be equipped with the capacity to listen to, and obey, the ten thousand demands and commandments hidden in the ten thousand situations with which life is confronting him. And it is these demands that are passed on to him by an alert conscience. Only then, by virture of an alert conscience, can he also resist the effects of the existential vacuum, namely, conformism and totalitarianism.

Meaning must be found and cannot be given. And it must be found by oneself, by one's own conscience. To give meanings would amount to moralizing. But I for one think that if morals are to survive they have to be ontologized. Ontologized morals, however, will no longer define what is good and what is bad in terms of what one should do over against what one must not do, respectively. But what is good will be defined as that which fosters the meaning fulfillment of a being. And what is bad will be defined as that which hinders this meaning fulfillment.

In addition to being ontologized, morals are to be existentialized as well. A doctor cannot give meanings to his patients. Nor can a professor give meanings to his students. What he may give, however, is an example, the existential example of his personal commitment to the search for truth. As a matter of fact the answer to the question what is the meaning of life can only be given out of one's whole being — his own life is the answer to the question of its meaning.

Human existence is characterized by self-transcendence rather than self-actualization. Man is characterised by his "search for meaning" rather than his "search for himself." Just as self-actualization can be obtained only on a detour, namely, through meaning fulfillment, likewise identity is available only through responsibility, through being responsible for the fulfillment of meaning. Research conducted at Boston University based on a new test that "measures the collective neurosis as formulated by" logotherapy, even "shows that there appears to be a negative correlation between the collective neurosis and responsibility."[26]

Humanness is characterized by responsibleness.[20] Man is responsible for fulfilling the meaning of his life. Being human means responding to life situations, replying to the questions they ask. Being human means answering these calls. Who is calling? To whom is man responding? These questions cannot be answered by logotherapy. It is the patient who must answer them. Logotherapy cannot but heighten the patient's awareness of his responsibleness. And responsibleness includes being responsible for one's answer to the question how to intepret his life, that is to say, whether along the lines of theism or atheism.

From this it follows that logotheraphy is a far cry from "taking over the patient's responsibility and diminishing him as a person."[27] By the same token, logotherapy does not "hover close to authoritarianism."[27] It is not a logotherapist but rather the psychoanalist who "is a moralist first and foremost,"[28] to quote from the *International Journal of Psycho-Analysis*. And it is not logotherapy but rather psycho-analysis that is defined by E. Mansell Pattison as "a moral enterprise whose central concern is morality."[29] To quote, for a change, representatives of behavior therapy, L. Krasner states that "it is the therapist who is making decisions as to what is good and bad behavior,"[30] Joseph Wolpe and Arnold A. Lazarus even "do not shrink from attacking on rational grounds a patient's religious beliefs if they are a source of suffering."[31]

Logotherapy can be defined as education to responsibility.[32,33] Today and at present responsibility, in turn, must be defined as selectivity. We are living in an affluent society. However, affluence not only concerns material goods but there is also an affluence of various sorts of stimuli. We are bombarded by the mass media. We are bombarded by sexual stimulation. And, last but not least, there is an affluence in the sense of the information explosion. Heaps of books and journals pile up on our desks. Unless we wish to drown in total (not only sexual) promiscuity, we have to choose between what is important and what is not, what is meaningful and what is not. We have to become selective and discriminate.

When addressing the 1967 Conference of College Presidents which was sponsored by the Institute of Higher Education of Teachers College, Columbia University, I concluded by saying: "I venture to predict here and now the surge of a new sense of responsibleness." The rise of this responsibleness is noticeable particularly among the youth. I see its first signs in the protest movements, although I must frankly confess that much of this protesting is better described as antitesting because it is not struggling *for* something but rather *against* something. But this is quite understandable because the young people are caught in the existential vacuum. They do not know anything worthy of being fought for, and there are so many things to be against. However, I am sure that sooner or later they will come up with the positive, constructive, creative alternatives. This should not be difficult. After all, a lot of tasks are in store for them, waiting for being completed by them. They just have to widen and broaden their horizon and then will notice that there is plenty of meaning to fulfill around them.

This would entail and engender a sense of co-responsibleness. In Canada last Winter certain students were fasting, and citizens were invited to pay a certain amount for each hours that a student went without food. The students sent the money to Biafra. At the same time we had a lot of snow in Vienna. There was a labor shortage because so few people cared to do the menial labor of shoveling snow. Students from the University of Vienna volunteered to do the work and sent that money to Biafra too. In this I see an example of a growing concern with other people on a planetary level, an increasing sense of world-wide solidarity.

The psychiatrist or, for that matter, the logotherapist cannot show his patient *what* the meaning is.[21] Even less can he "supply the patient with his goal."[27] But he may well show the patient that *there is* a meaning and, what is even more important, that life not only holds a meaning — a unique meaning — for each and every man but also never ceases to hold such a meaning, it retains it, it remains meaningful literally up to its last moment, to his last breath. This is due to the fact that even the negative, tragic aspects of human existence or what I call the tragic triad — pain, guilt and death — may be turned into something positive, into something creative. Caught in a hopeless situation as its helpless victim, facing a fate that cannot be changed, man still may turn his predicament into an achievement and accomplishment at the human level. He thus may bear witness to the human potential, he may turn tragedy into a triumph. "The measure of a man is the way he bears up under misfortune," as Plutarch once put it.

Here we do not at all embark on value judgments on facts but rather on factual statements on values, we analyze the valuing process as it goes on in the unbiased man in the street whenever he sets out to find the meaning of his life. The unbiased man in the street does not understand himself in terms of being the battleground on the clashing claims of ego, id and superego. Nor does he understand himself in terms of a pawn and plaything of conditioning processes or drives and instincts.[33] By virtue of the ontological self-understanding or what is called the wisdom of the heart he knows that being human means being responsible for fulfilling the meaning potential inherent in a given life situation. And knows that meaning may not only be found in creating a work and doing a deed, not only in encountering someone and experiencing something but also, if need be, in the way in which he stands up to suffering.

As we see, the unbiased analysis of the unbiased man in the street reveals how he actually experiences values. Such an analysis is a phenomenological analysis. It refrains from any preconceived patterns of interpretation and abstains from forcing the phenomena into the Procrustean bed of one's pet concepts along the lines of his particular indoctrination, pet concepts such as "underlying psychodynamics" or "operant conditioning."

The phenomenological analysis of the man in the street yields those immediate data of experience from which an axiology may be distilled. More specifically, three chief groups of values may be discerned. I have classified them in terms of creative, experiential and attitudinal values.[20] And the phenomenological analysis of the wisdom of the heart on the part of the man in the street reveals and discloses that he is cognizant of this trichotomy. In addition, however, he knows that attitudinal values rank higher than creative and experiential values. In other words, he also is cognizant of this hierarchy. Research based on computerized data obtained from 1,340 subjects has offered statistical evidence for, both, the trichotomy of values and their hierarchy.[7]

As I see it, it is the assignment of phenomenology to translate the wisdom of the heart into scientific terms. From this it follows that if morals are to survive they have not only to be ontologized and existentialized but also phenomenologized. The man in the street is the true teacher of morals. Let me illustrate this by a write-up on the seminars at the University of Chicago's Billings Hospital:

"Unseen behind a one-way glass, medical students, social workers, nurses and aides, chaplains and student chaplains watch sufferers from illnesses which most often are fatal come to an understanding with death. In an entirely real sense, the patients are teachers — through their own experience — about the end of life" (*Life* magazine).

A sense of fulfillment is available to the man in the street, indeed, in the face of dying — and suffering. To demonstrate this let me take up a letter I received from Florida State Prison, more specifically, Number 020640:

"At the age of 54, financially ruined, in jail, I have undergone a tremendous recovery. This happened in the stillness of my cell, I am at complete peace with myself and the world.

I have found the true meaning of my life, and time can only delay its fulfillment but not deter it. How wonderful life is, I embrace today, anxiously await tomorrow."

The self-understanding consists of two aspects: "a prelogical understanding of being" and "a pre-moral understanding of meaning."[35] In some cases, both aspects are repressed. They are not compatible with the indoctrination along the lines of a reductionist philosophy of life. This results in nihilism against which a reaction formation is built up, namely, cynicism. I once had to take over the treatment of an outstanding psychoanalyst who was caught in a severe depression resulting from nihilism. It was hard to have him find his way to the existential ground on which the direction and vision of values again was available to him because he — *was* the direction and vision.

Even in nihilists the wisdom of the heart may supersede the knowledge of the brain and allow for recognizing the unconditional meaningfulness of life by virtue of the potential meaning of suffering. "It is strange," a graduate psychology student of the University of California in Berkeley writes in a letter to me. "The nihilists first laugh at your concept of meaning through suffering — and ultimately their tears dissolve them."

To repeat my contention: phenomenology means translating this wisdom of the heart into scientific terms — and to add another one: logotherapy means retranslating it into plain words, into the language of the man in the street so that he again may benefit from it. And it is possible to put it across to him. Let me just recall what happened when I once addressed the prisoners of San Quentin in California at the request of this prison's director. After I had addressed these prisoners who were the toughest criminals in California, one prisoner stood up and said, "Dr. Frankl, would you be kind enough to say a few words through the mike to Aaron Mitchell, who is expecting his death in the gas chamber in a couple of days. The people from Death Row are not allowed to come down to the Chapel, but perhaps you will say a few words particularly to him." (An embarrassing situation, but I had to take this challenge and say a few words.) I improvisingly said, "Mr. Mitchell, believe me, I understand your situation. I myself had to live for some time in the shadow of a gas chamber. But believe me, even then I did not give up my conviction of the unconditional meaningfulness of life, because either life has a meaning — then it must retain this meaning even if it is shortly lived; or life has no meaning — then just adding ever more years and perpetuating this meaningless job could not be of any meaning either. And believe me, even a life that has been meaningless all along, and that has been wasted, may — even in the last moment — be bestowed with meaning by the way in which we tackle this situation." And I told him the story that is laid down in Leo Tolstoy's novel *The Death of Ivan Ilyich* — the story of a man who is about 60 years of age and suddenly comes to know that he is to die in a couple of days. But by the insight he gains not only in this fact but in the fact that he had wasted his life, that his life had been virtually meaningless — by the insight he gains, he rises above himself, he grows beyond himself and thereby finally becomes capable of retroactively flooding his life with infinite meaningfulness. And believe me, this message came across.[36]

Let us return to the feeling of meaninglessness and resume discussing it. To quote Albert Einstein, "the man who regards his life as meaningless is not merely unhappy but hardly fit for life." Indeed, survival is dependent on direction. However, survival cannot be the supreme value. Unless life points to something beyond itself, survival is pointless and meaningless. It is not even possible. This is the lesson I have learned in 3 years spent in Auschwitz and Dachau, and it has been confirmed by psychiatrists in prisoner of war camps. Only those who were oriented toward the future were likely to survive toward a goal in the future, toward a meaning to fulfill in the future. And I think that this is not only true of the survival of individuals but also holds for the survival of mankind.

It is obvious that the subject boils down to an axiological issue. Are there values shared by people and peoples? Are there common denominators as to what they feel makes their lives worth living?

The only thing I know for sure is that if common values and meanings are to be found, what is due is another step to take, after mankind thousands of years ago developed monotheism, the belief in the one God. It is not enough, it will not do. What we need is not only the belief in the one God but also the awareness of the one mankind, the awareness of the unit of humanity. I would call it — mon-anthropism.

Endnotes

1. Viktor E. Frankl: *Man's Search for Meaning*. New York: Washington Square Press, 1963.
2. Personal communication received from Ing. Alois Habinger.
3. Louis L. Klitzke: "Students in Emerging Africa: Humanistic Psychology and Logotherapy in Tanzania," *American Journal of Humanistic Psychology*, 9 (1969), pp. 105-26.
4. Osvald Vymetal: *Acta Universitatis Palackianae Olumucensis*, 43 (1966), pp. 265-88.
5. James C. Crumbaugh and Leonard T. Maholick: "An Experimental Study in Existentialism: The Psychometric Approach to Frankl's Concept of Noogenic Neurosis," *Journal of Clinical Psychology*, 20 (1964), pp. 200-7.
6. James C. Crumbaugh: "Cross Validation of Purpose-in-Life Test Based on Frankl's Concepts," *Journal of Individual Psychology*, 24 (1968), pp. 74-81.
7. Elisabeth S. Lukas: A Dissertation, University of Vienna, 1970.
8. R. N. Gray: "An Analysis of Physicians' Attitudes of Cynicism and Humanitarianism before and after Entering Medical Practice," *J. Med. Educat.*, 40 (1955), p. 760.
9. Joseph Wilder: "Values and Psychotheraphy," *American Journal of Psychotherapy*, 23 (1969), p. 405.
10. Julius Heuscher: "Book Review," *Journal of Existentialism*, 5 (1964), p. 229.
11. Edith Weisskopf-Joelson: "Relative Emphasis on Nine Values by a Group of College Students," *Psychological Reports*, 24 (1969), p. 299.
12. Viktor E. Frankl: Beyond Self-Actualization and Self-Expression," *Journal of Existential Psychiatry*, 1 (1960), pp. 5-20.
13. Abraham H. Maslow: *Eupsychian Management*. Homewood: Irwin, 1965.

14. James C. Crumbaugh and Leonard T. Maholick: "The Case for Frankl's Will to Meaning," *Journal of Existential Psychiatry*, 4 (1963), pp. 43-8.

15. Rolf von Eckartsberg: *Introduction to Experiential Social Psychology*. Patmos III Publications, Vol. I, Spring, 1969.

16. Abraham H. Maslow: "Comments on Dr. Frankl's Paper," *Readings in Humanistic Psychology*, edited by Anthony J. Sutich and Miles A. Vich. New York: The Free Press, 1969.

17. S. Kratochvil and I. Planova: Unpublished paper.

18. Theodore A. Kotchen: "Existential Mental Health," *Journal of Individual Psychology*, 16 (1960), 174.

19. Annemarie von Forstmeyer: A Dissertation, United States International University, 1970.

20. Viktor E. Frankl: *The Doctor and the Soul*. New York: Bantam Books, 1969.

21. Viktor E. Frankl: *The Will to Meaning*. New York: New American Library, 1970.

22. Abraham H. Maslow: *Religions, Values, and Peak Experiences*. Columbus: Ohio State University Press, 1964.

23. Robert Athanesiou, Phillip Shaver and Carlo Tavris: "A Psychology Today Report on 20,000 Responses to 101 Questions about Sexual Attitudes and Practices," *Psychology Today*, 4 (1970), pp. 37-52.

24. Viktor E. Frankl: *Psychotherapy and Existentialism*. New York: Simon and Schuster, 1968.

25. Max Wertheimer: "Some Problems in the Theory of Ethics," *Documents of Gestalt Psychology*. edited by M. Henle. Berkeley: University of California Press, 1961.

26. Personal communication received from Professor Orlo Strunk, Jr.

27. Rollo May: *Existential Psychology*. New York: Random House, second edition, 1969.

28. Gordon F. Pleune: "All Dis-Ease Is Not Disease," *International Journal of Psycho-Analysis*, 46 (1965), 358.

29. Mansell E. Pattison: "Ego Morality," *Psychoanal, Rev.*, 55 (1968), pp. 187-222, quoted from *Digest of Neurology and Psychiatry*, 36 (1968).

30. L. Krasner: Quoted from David Grossman: "Of Whose Unscientific Methods and Unaware Values?" *Psychotherapy: Theory, Research and Practice*, 5 (1968), 53.

31. Joseph Wolpe and Arnold A. Lazarus: *Behavior Therapy Techniques*. Long Island City: Pergamon Press.

32. Karl Dienelt: *Von Freud zu Frankl*. Wien: Osterreichischer Bundesverlag, 1967.

33. Joseph D. Fabry: *The Pursuit of Meaning: Logotherapy Applied to Life*. Boston: Beacon Press, 1969.

34. Viktor E. Frankl: "Determinism and Humanism." *Humanitas*,

1971.
35. Viktor E. Frankl: *The Unconscious God*. New York: Washington Square Press, 1971.
36. Viktor E. Frankl: *The Existential Vacuum: A Challenge to Psychiatry*. San Francisco: Lodestar Press, 1971.

PART III

EAST-WEST AND VALUES

Values in a Marxist Perspective

Roger Garaudy

The basic thesis of Marxism with regard to the problem of value is that labor is the source of all value. The labor theory of value is but a particular case of this philosophical concept. In *Das Kapital*, labor in its specifically human form is distinguished from animal labor by the fact that human labor is preceeded by consciousness of ends. With the birth of man came the appearance of project — of finality. Man is always something other and more than the result or the product of historical conditions that gave birth to him. Thus, in the actions of man, as the criterion of his value, there is affirmed the moment of subjectivity and the moment of transcendence — the criterion of creativeness. This explains the watchword that Lenin gave to every revolutionary worthy of the name — one must dream — for the revolution is never born solely of determinism from the past. It requires the creative initiative of men.

Marxism is firstly the methodology of this historic initiative. The appearance of project and finality breaks the animal circle of instinct and permits recourse to tools. Labor is thus both an exteriorization of man and a humanization of nature. Through the labor of man things are transformed into objects answering human purposes. In thus modifying nature, man himself is changed, for the creation of these objects arouses new needs in him, and widens the scope of his power and of his desires. The second criterion of value after the criterion of creativeness is therefore the criterion of efficiency: man's greater mastery of nature, of himself and of his own history.

The labor of man is always social labor. Even if the individual works alone, there lives in him the knowledge and the technique of the entire human species in the full development of its history. As soon as labor reaches a certain degree of complexity — as, for example, with the settling of the land and the birth of agriculture — a division of labor becomes a necessary condition to its progress. This division of labor leads in its turn to a division in the classes — master and slave, feudal lord and serf, employer and worker — in which the owner of the means of production has the privilege of determining the purposes of the labor. The owner thus deprives the worker, who does not own the means of production, whether the worker be slave, serf, or laborer, of the specifically human character of his work. That is to say, the owner prevents the worker from the setting of objectives and thus brings about a fundamental alienation of the working man, his disassociation and his mutilation. These production relationships or class relationships and the political relationships sanctioned by them — the principal function of the state for a Marxist being the maintenance by force or repression of existing social relationships — enjoy a relative autonomy with regard to the present condition of productive forces and techniques. The form of the state can lag behind the productive forces as, for instance, was the case with the French monarchy just before the French revolution, and will thereby act as a brake on development. The criterion of value respecting production in the state is, in this case, a criterion of correspondence. Man's consciousness of his creative work and of his alienation, of his technical powers and of his political and social relationships, lies at the religious, moral, philosophical and esthetic levels, where man's values, modes of behavior and thought with regard to the outside world are determined.

Here two fundamental errors are to be avoided if the Marxist theory of value is to make progress. The first error consists in a manner widespread nowadays in opposing ideology to theory. In the thought of Marx, ideology is not the contrary of theory. It is its prehistoric period. A particular proof is thus on the one hand relative, in that it will be historically out-distanced by a more general theory of which it will be but a particular case; for instance, the geometry of

Euclid with regard to later non-Euclidian geometry, or classical mechanics in comparison with quantum mechanics. And on the other hand, this proof is *absolute* to the extent that the powers over nature it has given to us shall become a part of the new theory that will deny it, absorb it, and go beyond it, in accordance with the writ of Hegelian dialectics.

The second error to be avoided is reducing faith, especially religious faith, to an ideology. Faith is not a manner of interpreting the outside world but a mode of behavior towards it and living in resignation or in refusal and creation. The criterion of the value of an ideology — a theory or a faith — at the religious, philosophical, moral or esthetic level, is essentially the criterion of transcendence. Thus it maintains the creative moment of the project — its aptitude for criticism of the datum and anticipation of the purposes in the name of which man is striving to transform it. Thus it safeguards the universal aim through which the real historical possibility of participation in such a project is not reserved to a group, or a so-called elite, but to all men. Thus it leaves to man, against alienation to some sort of destiny, full responsibility for his history.

This concept acknowledges the plurality and the autonomy of values and their criteria. It can be lived as a religion or in atheism: that is, as a presence — a code, a hope — or, on the contrary, as an absence — an experience of the impossibility of closing the system, together with the possibility of an opening to any other system. The common denominator is a certainty that man is too great to be self-sufficient. Alienation in the Marxist usage of the term is the contrary of creation. It reduces value to the level of an act — positivism of values. Labor is alienated when the worker, manual or intellectual, is dispossessed of the possibility of determining or questioning, the objectives and the meaning. Protestation against this mutilation of the specifically human act of labor was, in May, 1969 in Paris, the common denominator of the aspirations of the students and the claims of the workers. It was the center of the project of socialism with a human face, worked out by the Communists and the people of Czechoslovakia, from January to August, 1969.

The alienation of social relationships and political relationships is given concrete expression in all forms of exploitation of men by men and of domination in national oppression through colonialism and neocolonialism. Tied, in its very principle to any regime based on a mercantile economy and the class system, alienation does not disappear spontaneously when a socialist regime is set up. Not only does the survival of a mercantile economy permit roots aiming at the alienation of labor to subsist, but the organizing of forms of planification and of a centralized dictatorial and bureaucratic state, create specific forms of alienation. In Capitalist as in Socialist countries, alienation stems from a reduction in values for the benefit of a single one of them. In Capitalist countries, generally speaking, it is the primacy of productive powers that is over-estimated. The result is a conception of social life and its values reduced to the single imperative of growth. Such growth for growth's sake, such a religion of means, leads to a reduction and an integration of all other values. An eminent American economist has summed up this tendency in the following story: "to lead souls to leaven or hell — it is as if St. Peter had a single criterion: What have you done in your life to increase the Gross National Product?"

The basic problem posed by the countries of the Third World in the dialogue of civilizations lies in the plurality of development criteria — economic growth being not the sole, nor perhaps the most important criterion, and the choice of means and values being in the nature of a question rather than of an answer. In Socialist countries, it is generally the primacy of the production relationship that is over-estimated. The postulate has too long been accepted according to which the exploitation of man by man being abolished, a new man should necessarily, automatically, be born of this revolution in class relationships.

Furthermore, since Socialism was set up initially in countries with a heavy legacy of underdevelopment, interference between the problem of coping with underdevelopment and that or erecting the socialist structure called for an extreme concentration of resources and power, with all that it entailed in violations of socialist democracy in the states and the parties, and the reduction of all values to a single one: the imperativè need to catch up with the technical and the economic advance of the foremost capitalistic countries. From that moment and for a long period, everything that led to this objective was true, good, and fine. This vital requirement implied logical, moral and esthetic standards, and also implied degeneracy: dialectics ceasing to be an instrument of research and becoming a justifying ideology; moral standards placing unilateral emphasis on discipline and the respect for rules, to the detriment of the critical faculty and creativeness; art being considered from a short term, utilitarian viewpoint, and not as a continued creation of man by man, as the creation of the creative man. Reduction of values, social integration and the religion of means taken as ends, have led, during the past few years, to a general contestation of values by the younger generation who no longer accept being made part of a system without judging its aims, its meanings, its values. Even if the form taken by this protestation varied greatly according as it occurred in a capitalist country, a socialist country, or a country of the Third World — even if its external expression has often been utopian, destructive, anarchistic, the underlying reason for this explosion is common to all continents and all systems.

The great scientific and technical mutation of the cybernetization of both production and management is a principle of the new contradictions that have brought about this world wide upheaval. The first industrial revolution with the steam engine and the triumph of machinery tended essentially towards an increase in the number and power of machines and of the labor necessary to serve them. The first form of industrialization also led to a subdivision of, and more and more searching analysis of, labor until man was turned into an appendix of the machine, and the subjectivity of a victim. Marx, in *Das Kapital*, studied the various aspects of what he called in the language of Classical German philosophy, the inversion of subject and object: the basic alienation of the subject to the object. Thus the working man became a thing among other things — a cog in the wheel. The technical mutation following the cybernetization of production and management at present make possible a new inversion. The tendency towards de-qualification constant for the past century and a half is being reversed. The number of skilled workers, of technicians, engineers and supervisory personnel, is henceforward increasing faster than that of unskilled labor. The very notion of professional qualification has changed. An increasing number of workers are required to have an over all synthetic grasp of the technological process in its entirety — an aptitude to pose problems, and the need to take frequent refresher courses because of rapid improvement of techniques. General culture thus plays an increasing part in professional qualification.

A similar phenomenon occurs at the level of management. Whereas half a century ago the greatest earning power went to a maximum concentration of initiative and decision, what appears to have a steadily increased earning power today in the most advanced and highly cybernetized sectors, is a reduction in number of the centers of initiative and decision. Thus, at both management and production levels, present technical developments require the transition from a rationality of the mechanical type to one of the cybernetic type — substituting the feed-back of initiative at the base, for the manipulation of men considered as things and disregarding their subjectivity. When one imagines from Wells to Orwell that the future of man is necessarily that of a robot, when we are presented with this future in the form, for instance, given to it in a Bradbury novel or in Truffaut's film *Fahrenheit 451*, we are not dealing with an anticipation of the future but with an extrapolation of the past.

The greatest error would be to have men imitate the machine, when the cybernetic mutation opens the way to an unprecedented blossoming of human subjectivity. The false prophets of the death of man who in the name of an abstract and doctrinaire structuralism, define man as a marionette whose strings are pulled by structures (as said my friend, Altuseir) are theorizing on what is already in the past of man and his former failures. Let the dead bury the dead.

The new scientific and technical revolution requires, in reply, the most radical revolution in the history of man. In the first place, because the very ends of culture are displaced, henceforward, at the heart of material production and not on its fringes there can develop for steadily increasing numbers of men aptitudes for synthesis, renovation and questioning, that formerly characterized the culture of humanist elite. Culture of the specifically human dimension of man becomes the first condition of development in all the senses of the word. Everything that religion and art have placed beyond labor, outside it, with doubled man becomes a center — chiefly the specifically human dimension of subjectivity and transcendence. Today then the problem is to reconquer — in what has been called the unidimensional societies which reduce values — all the lost dimensions.

At the present stage — one of cybernetics and the development of productive forces — it becomes a steadily growing contradiction to ask of man a maximum of initiative, of responsibility, even of creativeness in his professional task, and at the same time to require of him unconditional obedience to the owner, individual or collective, of the means of production. This contradiction tends to become the major contradiction of our times. Marxism, I have said, is a methodology of historical initiatives that permits us to draw out of present contradictions the possible future capital of overcoming them. At a time when the very demands of the development of science, of technique, and of the economy, create the conditions for this explosion of subjectivity, this affirmation of man's transcendence with regard to the overall condition of his existence sets the concrete problem of value in terms that meet the correspondence criterion: establish social relationships permitting the full expansion of this possibility. In other words, make of man, and of every man, a man: a creator at all levels of his social existence at the economic, political and cultural levels. Such, in my opinion, is the first task at this close of the twentieth century, of the concrete philosophy of values: establish social relationships corresponding to the level of development of the productive forces in order to create the conditions fostering the blooming of the new man, who has to be taught to come to life: first a militant of the revolt against all alienations; second, a poet of creativeness against entropy.

Chinese Values: The China Problem and our Problem

Wm. Theodore de Bary

China's massive size and potential power are unquestionably of fundamental significance in understanding the "China problem." But they are not new phenomena. In the sixteenth or eighteenth centuries China was in its own way powerful and its people represented an even larger proportion of the world's population than they do today. Yet recognition of these facts by the West at that time did not suffice to establish the diplomatic relations Westerners then so eagerly desired. Something more was involved than simply recognizing the size and power of China, something to do with the attitudes and institutions of the Chinese themselves. Failing to reckon adequately with the latter, impatient Westerners have diagnosed China according to their own experience and values rather than those of the Chinese, and have sought to impose or connive at what they could not achieve by persuasion.

The ancient Chinese philosopher Chuang Tzu told many fables and parables exposing the human tendency to impose one's own values on others, and to assume that they should want to be like us. He was amused that man should be so ready to generalize and to judge from his own limited experience, and so prone to being misled by even his own generous impulses. A favourite story of mine has to with "boring holes in chaos."

"The sovereign of the Southern Sea is called Dissatisfaction [with things as they are] ; the Sovereign of the Northern Sea, Revolution; the Sovereign of the Centre of the World, Chaos.

Dissatisfaction and Revolution from time to time met together in the territory of Chaos, and Chaos treated them very
hospitably. The two sovereigns planned how to repay Chaos's
kindness. They said, 'Men all have seven holes to their bodies
for seeing, hearing, eating, and breathing. Our friend has none
of these. Let us try to bore some holes in him.' Each day
they bored one hole. On the seventh day Chaos died."

There are some delightful ironies in this fable, and parallels
both to modern China and to our relations with her. May not
our insistent attempts to open China, whether in the nineteenth century or more recently, be something like trying to
bore holes in Chaos? Isn't it possible that China feels no need
to be opened? May not her experience of being forcibly
entered in the nineteenth century, and then of being help-
lessly exposed to the outside world in earlier decades of this
century, have convinced the Chinese that they were right in
the first place and can do without contacts of that kind?
Should we not consider the possibility that whatever we
might think about the desirability of "normal," that is, open
relations with China, the Chinese may prefer them to be
much more closed? Should we not try to reexamine international relations from a Chinese perspective, and especially
from the perspective of Chinese history? That history, and
the basic character of Chinese life, have been different
enough from ours so that the common assumptions and
expectations of most Americans — from political right to
left — do not apply.

I shall take the risk, then, of offering some rather large
generalizations about the historical experience of the Chinese.
China's long history, like that of other major Asian civilizations, can be characterized as introverted and intensive in its
development, as compared to that of the West which has
been more extroverted and extensive. In general, Western
civilizations have tended to look outward on the world and
Asian civilizations to look inward. Traditional Chinese
society was land-based and oriented to the territory we
speak of as "China Proper," in contrast to Western civilizations which were oriented first to the Mediterranean, then
the Atlantic and finally the Pacific — and also in contrast

to Japan, which always had a maritime orientation. To say that China was land-based is to say that it was earthbound, that is, it depended on the "good earth" for the support of its dense population — a density that was of modern proportions since before the time of Christ. (China has faced the problem of the modern population explosion throughout most of its history.)

Chinese dynasties, essentially concerned with control and management of land, worked out an elaborate system of control under a bureaucratic state, based primarily on military control of the land, political control of the peasants working it, and fiscal control of their production in the form of land and produce taxes that supported the ruling class.

On the whole, China's historical achievement in coping with these problems has been impressive, but it has not been without certain costs by Western standards. Typically the Chinese state, when ever it had the power to do so, tried to keep the population fixed on the land so as to maximise agricultural production. It restricted freedom of movement within China and tried to prevent travel outside. These restrictions made it difficult even for Buddhist monks to go to India or Japan. Greater freedom of travel became possible only when state control weakened; political disintegration was the price of greater freedom of movement. Chinese dynasties tended to see the outside world, not as a field of potential exploration and economic development, but as simply insignificant or valueless. As rulers of the Central Kingdom, their only concern was with the security of their borders, without any intrusion from outside that might threaten the peace and stability of those within or jeopardize their own control over the land.

Out of its preoccupation with land and agriculture, the state regarded commercial and industrial activities as diversionary and the incipient middle class as parasitic, if not actually pernicious in its influence. The bureaucratic elite, or Mandarin class, gave little thought to economic development, but rather extended to commerce and industry essentially the same static, regulatory policy that had characterized its control of the land and agriculture. Hence,

the economic dynamism that emerged out of Western feudal
society did not develop in China. Commercial expansion,
industrial investment, maritime enterprise, and the accumula-
tion of private capital were greatly inhibited. The characteristic Chinese method of dealing with foreign trade and
intercourse was to restrict it to one or two ports where it
could be closely watched and controlled by officials, so that
profits could be taxed and exposure to outside influences
strictly curtailed.

On the above points there are both similarities and differences between traditional and Communist China, but I
should say that in essential respects they remain the same. By
this I do not mean that China is simply unchanging, but only
that it changes more slowly than most people think, and that
the change conforms more to established patterns and
preferences than many realize. For instance, in this century
there has been a notable shift in the attitude of China's
leaders toward economic development and an awareness of
the need to stimulate it. But in spite of Mao's frantic efforts
to industrialize in the fifties, the mismanagement and failures
of the Great Leap Forward have forced the Chinese Communist leadership to recognize the primacy of agricultural
production and give more attention to strengthening agriculture as a precondition for industrial advance. As of now,
nothing has happened to alter the basic facts of Chinese
economic life in this respect. China remains primarily an
agricultural country with the same dependence on the land
as before, with the overwhelming majority of the population
remaining peasants. The implications of this fact for the
Chinese way of life, for the attitudes and values of most
Chinese, are tremendous.

Another way of looking at this problem is to consider
the intellectual and educational needs of a modern China
supposedly committed to large scale industrialization and
technological change. To accomplish this it would seem
essential that education and scientific training be given high
priority, and many persons have supposed that this would
inevitably lead to a loosening of ideology, a liberalization in
thought, and a general mellowing of the system. Yet the

Cultural Revolution has shown how the commitment to scientific and technical training is highly qualified by the demands of ideological discipline, and how educational institutions could be closed for long periods in the higher interests of political mobilization. I would not suggest that this is a peculiarly Chinese phenomenon, but I think it may be said that a traditional Chinese moralistic approach to politics has contributed to the bizarre manifestations and peculiar intensity of the struggles that arose from the Cultural Revolution, all of which have seriously hampered China's scientific and technological development.

Nevertheless China has not abandoned the aim of industrializing, and for this a far greater involvement in foreign trade is called for than China has traditionally engaged in. The sizeable trade with Japan, for instance, despite Japan's political unacceptability and refusal to submit to Peking's preconditions for diplomatic relations, attests to a dependence by China on outside sources quite in contrast to her traditional self-sufficiency. Yet at the same time Peking relies on agricultural exports to pay for imports, and thus is compelled again to recognize the continuing primacy and priority of agriculture in the Chinese economy. A rising population, which makes ever increasing demands on food production, provides another reason why the Chinese Communist regime must give first attention to improving the condition of agriculture. In these circumstances foreign involvements and opportunities must still be subordinated to the age-old problems of internal production, internal stability, and internal security.

These developments have only confirmed a pattern of Chinese foreign relations strikingly similar to the traditional one. Before the Nixon-Mao meetings the basic pattern was one of distinctly limited engagement in diplomatic and cultural intercourse. Among the signs of this were the steady reduction in the number of foreign consulates in China; the refusal of Peking to participate in international meetings to which Chinese were invited; the tight control over Chinese students abroad, lest they be contaminated by contact with other students (even Communist students in Moscow and

Eastern Europe); or, conversely, the close surveillance of foreign students in Peking and the severe restriction of their movements and contacts with the Chinese people. Long ago Khrushchev complained that it had become impossible to carry on any kind of fraternal relations and friendly exchanges between individual Chinese and Soviet party members. Western newsmen in Peking have reported on the extreme difficulty of establishing any contacts there; they have felt more isolated from the news in the Chinese capital than they have in Hongkong. The recent shift in Peking's policy, post-Mao, offers the prospect of increased contacts, but without any evidence of radical change in this basic pattern. Indeed foreign policy reorientations are probably predicated on the assumption that they need not disturb the internal pattern too greatly.

As for our relations with China, we must remind ourselves of the inevitable distortion that arises from looking at her too much in terms of how she relates to us. This is not a matter of high priority for them. The life of China goes on largely oblivious of us. Its leaders have other urgent problems and more immediate concerns. We remain on the periphery of their vision, unless and until some other factor intervenes to turn their attention our way, to make them take us into account.

As an example of the difference between China's attitude and ours, we may take the question of her participation in world organizations. For us the United Nations represents the ultimate effort to extend the basic principles of Western political democracy on a global scale by establishing a world-wide system of consultation and representative government. Our extensive concept of universality demands that it be as inclusive as possible, even of disparate elements. Hence our discomfort at the absence of Red China. The Chinese experience, however, does not conform to this pattern. In its several thousand years of history up to the end of the ninth century, China had never known a system of parliamentary government or even the advocacy of one. Considering the maturity of China's social development, the millions of Chinese who have survived without the benefits of parliamentarism, and the fact that their historical experience has not led them inevitably to it, we realize how far from being universal are our own concepts of universality. In traditional China universality would have been sought by having all peoples reach down further into the roots of their common human nature, rather than by trying to tie all of their organizational branches together.

In any case, the rejection of liberal democracy and parliamentarism has been a matter of conscious principle, reaffirmed again and again by Communist leaders. Anti-parliamentarism has been a major theme of Maoist propaganda and indoctrination during the Cultural Revolution. Mao himself possessed sufficient insight into Western liberalism to be aware of our dilemma and our discomfort. It was not he who agitated for China's admission to the U.N. He left that to Western liberals. Still we need not surrender all hope that these divergent attitudes, Western and Chinese, may some day converge. For the present, however, we should be under no illusions that the difference between the two is superficial and easily resolved. Admission of Red China to the U.N. has been a formality which has not led to any extensive participation in its parliamentary processes.

It is in the sphere of ideology that we encounter seemingly the sharpest break between China's past and present, and the greatest difficulty in discerning any continuity with traditional values. Of the major thought systems, Buddhism and Taoism largely disqualified themselves in matters of state and foreign policy. In political and social matters Confucianism represented the dominant tradition. Though in some ways it served to moderate and soften the harsher features of the dynastic state, Confucianism offered no resistance to isolationist tendencies. This was due less to an attitude of self-sufficiency or complacency, as is usually supposed, than to a sense of active concern for the welfare of those within China's borders. Confucianism discouraged external adventures and encouraged a generally pacific attitude toward neighboring peoples. True it possessed a fundamental conviction in the superiority of Chinese civilization, but that rested on a faith in the underlying moral values of

Confucian culture. It called on the ruler to engage in constant self-examination of his moral position, not his power position. It reminded him (whenever it had the opportunity to do so) of his responsibilities to his own subjects, of the need to ease their burdens and secure their livelihood. Repeatedly in the Ming and Manchu dynasties Confucian advisers argued against investment in modern arms and weapons technology, which would only mean added expense and a further burden on the people. Their trust was in virtue and benevolence rather than in "power and plotting."

Under Mao, with the total eclipse and suppression of Confucianism as an active force, this element of idealism and restraint was removed. Its pacific influence is no longer exerted on China's rulers. On the contrary, the residual influence of Confucian moral striving was found unconsciously transmuted, rather than consciously exploited, in Mao's intense belief in the necessity for waging unending class struggle. Though expressed in orthodox Marxist terms, it is not difficult to see how fundamentally this represented a constant struggle between good and evil rather than between social or economic classes as defined by any traditional Marxist criteria. To a degree then, it reflects the strong moralistic strain in Chinese thought.

Since China was traditionally isolationist, she did not play a large political and military role in Asia. Most dynasties were expansionist in their early phase — in the sense of establishing the frontiers of China as far out as they could, so as to extend their control of the land and insulate themselves from external forces. The natural limits of this expansionist phase were set by the resistance of the non-Chinese people involved and the cost China's rulers were willing to pay internally in support of such moves. A preoccupation with internal problems usually led to the diminution of this outward thrust, and left China's immediate neighbors intact. Some weak or minority groups were enveloped within the Chinese Empire and very gradually or partially assimilated. But many other peoples numerically and culturally inferior to the Chinese maintained an independent or autonomous existence on China's borders down into modern times: Mongols, Manchus, Koreans, Ryukyuans, Taiwanese, Annemese, Thai, Burmese, and Tibetans. They might acknowledge for brief periods some vague suzerainty on the part of China, but they were politically and culturally autonomous. This reflects not only the inherent limits of Chinese dynastic expansion, but also the Confucian belief that cultural conversion, or the civilizing process, was incompatible with the use of force. If people did not spontaneously recognize the superiority of Chinese civilization, there were only two things to do: leave them alone, or examine one's own conduct to see why one had failed to command the respect and emulation of others.

Under Mao Chinese expansionism in East and South-East Asia was basically that of a traditional dynasty in its early phase, before natural limits or balance have been established. However, with the restraining influence of Confucianism gone, two new forms of expansionism or aggressiveness made their appearance.

First, in Tibet, where an autonomous culture and distinctive way of life had been maintained throughout the centuries into the mid-1950s, the Tibetans were forcibly converted to the Chinese way of life, and their own culture, based on Buddhism, was destroyed. From a technical standpoint, this may not be reckoned as "aggression" in international law. In modern times no one has disputed Chinese claims of suzerainty, and therefore resistance to forcible acculturation, even when it involves tremendous loss of life among the resisters, counts only as civil war. But in human and cultural values, this is an irreparable loss.

Second, with the Confucian struggle for self-control in the exercise of power superseded by the world revolutionary struggle of Communism, wars of liberation provided a means of extending Communist power that were not necessarily identifiable with the traditional kind of expansionism or ordinary military aggression. While Mao carried on his ideological offensive, communist China did not need to send troops beyond her borders in order to advance her cause in the world struggle for power. Through these means, nevertheless, she could hope to build a new Sino-centric world order.

   The eclipse of Mao's leadership put an end to these ambi-
tions, but even the present more benign attitude toward the
outer world is unlikely to alter the underlying pattern. China
is still subject to isolationist tendencies, of both a traditional
and a contemporary sort, which operate to keep China a
closed society. In Mao's role as defender of the orthodox
Communist tradition he could, on the one hand, shield
China from external influences and, on the other, assert his
ideological leadership throughout the world. This was shown
clearly in his isolating of the Chinese Communist Party from
incompatible forms of Communism and his unrelenting
suppression of heterodox and revisionist tendencies. Mao
therefore exercised the traditional ideological authority of
China's dynastic rulers at home, and in foreign affairs he
permitted active relations only with those subservient to his
own leadership. He related himself to and involved himself
in the outer world only to an extent compatible with the
preservation of China's isolation from external, non-
conformist, and potentially subversive influences.

   The recent campaign against liberalism and revisionism
during the Cultural Revolution represented both a rejection
of the bourgeois West and a traditional anti-foreignism,
essentially defensive and reactionary, shielding the Chinese
people from new influences and new options. It could not,
in the long run, succeed. Withdrawal and isolation from the
world could not solve Mao's problem because in fact he no
longer lived in the same world as the traditional dynasties.
His isolation was born in part of failure — not only the
immediate failures of the communes and the Great Leap
Forward, but through the prolonged difficulty China has
experienced in adjusting to a world of which China was not
the center, as Chinese have traditionally assumed. It was born
in part also of the shock that the Chinese suffered when their
own culture was largely uprooted by the storm of advancing
Western civilization and their traditional forms of education
were abruptly terminated in favor of some recent import
from Teacher's College or some idea issuing from the
Bolshevik revolution. Mao Tse-tung was the offspring of a
devastating assault on his mother culture. If we cannot

appreciate the depths of resentment and cultural shock that produced his hostility and intransigence, it is partly because we have never experienced anything like it in our own history.

Those who sympathized with Mao's predicament, or with his aims, were apt to justify his performance either on the ground that his economic failures were exaggerated in the West, or that they, as well as Mao's difficulties with the outside world, were really the consequence of our hostility and intransigence, not his. Whether or not such was the case, our expectations of changes now taking place should not take the misguided forms that Revolution and Dissatisfaction did in Chuang Tzu's parable, when they tried to bore holes in Chaos, thinking that he would be happier being like them. If one looks at the problem from the standpoint of Chinese history and the values of Chinese civilization, one need not believe that China's future well-being depends entirely on how successful it is in Westernizing. What absolute value attaches to industrialization in the Western style? Today we can understand better some of its unfortunate consequences and unanticipated side effects. Today we may be more ready to admit than we were, say in 1920, that we do not have the answers to all of our own problems, and that others may be able to avoid some of our mistakes if they can take the time to learn from them. A slower and more carefully considered program of industrialization might spare China some of the evils of pollution and urban decay. Even China's isolation may prove of some benefit if it insulates her people from some of the serious social problems that the supposed advance of Western civilization has brought in its wake.

I realize that this can be argued the other way around — that the delay in "modernizing" only postpones these problems instead of solving them; but I am willing to believe, nevertheless, that it may represent an eventual gain for world civilization if the Chinese can be left to work out these problems on their own, in keeping with their own circumstances and traditions. Much of China's anguish and distress in the recent past has arisen from her loss of self-respect in the nineteenth century and the attempt to efface its past in the twentieth century. This has left the Chinese with an

enormous problem: how to recover their own identity.
Significantly this was at issue in the Hai Jui case, over which
the Cultural Revolution broke out, for those attacked as
revisionists among the intellectuals were accused of adopting
a humanist philosophy as opposed to a class ideology and of
accepting certain fundamental human values as common to
China's past and present. That these were also Confucian
virtues, such as uprightness and outspoken honesty in officials, suggests the extremity of the crisis of values in contemporary China, as Maoism, twenty years after its seizure
of power, found that China's past still had the power to
attract thinking men.

As witnesses of these tragic struggles on the mainland of
China, we should have developed the capacity to see them,
not just in terms of the danger or advantage they presented
to us, but of how from these agonies China might be able to
regain her sense of self-respect.

In the reaction to Mao reflected in the ousting of the
"Gang of Four" we shall no doubt witness a swing of the
pedulum in the direction of greater willingness to learn from
the West. But once this reaction has subsided, if China
chooses to keep a certain distance between herself and us, we
must not think it either unnatural or intolerable. While the
slow process of adjustment goes on, we can begin adjusting
ourselves to a new world in which China will play its own
distinctive role. We can come to a better understanding of
both China's past and present, and to a better appreciation
of those values which she will eventually contribute to the
world community.

PART IV

VALUES AND THE ARTS

The Dilemma of Choosing: Speculations about Contemporary Culture

Leonard B. Meyer

Ours is a time of tension and turmoil. Apocalyptic anxieties press in upon us. The threat of nuclear holocaust, the population explosion, the destruction of our physical environment, the revolt of blacks against years of oppression, and the pervasive presence of violence both domestic and foreign — these formidable uncertainties form the foreground of our uncomfortable age.

And all seems to be foreground. Bombarded by the media, we are continually confronted by the insistent, instant tumult of today. The sounds and sights of the past are masked by the psychedelic blaze and blare of the oppressive present. The picture plane is flat and one-dimensional.

Without seeking to minimize the seriousness of our malignancies, I would suggest that if we want more than a "gut" reaction to the present — if we want to understand it — then we need the perspective which history provides. And history reminds us that whatever the peculiarities of our time may be, it is doubtful that existence today is more violent, confused and precarious than it was in earlier epochs. Think, for example, of the institutionalized cruelty of imperial Rome, of the personal violence of the Renaissance, and of the mass devastation of the Thirty Years War. Let us take two specific examples. Describing the life of a Lutheran scholar, who played a considerable role in the witch trials of the seventeenth century, H. R. Trevor-Roper observes:

. . . he would live to a ripe old age and look back on a meritorious life in the course of which he had read the Bible from cover to cover 53 times, taken the Sacrament every week, greatly intensified the methods and efficiency of torture, and procured the death of 20,000 persons.[1]

Coming closer to contemporary concerns, John Spiegel, a psychoanalyst and director of the Lomberg Center for the study of violence, has pointed out that there were bloody anti-Catholic riots in this country in the 1830s, anti-draft riots in the 1860s, labor riots in the 1870s, and anti-negro riots in the early part of this century. And, according to Spiegel, "Nothing that has happened in our cities since 1964 comes anywhere near the naked savagery of these previous outbreaks."[2]

The peculiarity of our period does not, I think, lie in the actual, quantitative level of its confusion, disruption and brutality. These may have been as high in the past. Rather our age is specially anxious, anguished and distraught because violence and disorder take place in an ideological climate which, generally speaking, has neither a coherent vision of the future, nor faith in the traditions of the past. We are literally disoriented. We don't know which way to turn. For if the implications of the present are unclear and the significance of the past seems uncertain, there is no rational basis for choosing among alternative courses of action.

The critical, the traumatic problem of our time is, I suggest, that of choosing — of making decisions in a complex, pluralistic culture which is without any general set of beliefs about the nature of man, his place in the universe, and the meaning of his existence. The problem is ubiquitous. It is everywhere in our culture — in the arts as well as in the area of social, political and economic events. Not only has the problem of choosing influenced our view of and response to the world around us, but, as I hope to show, it has played a significant role in shaping some aspects of contemporary behavior.

In what follows, I shall be explicitly concerned with the problem of choosing — and implicitly with the enigma of value — particularly as it arises in connection with the arts. Before turning to these matters, however, I should like to consider, if only briefly, the nature of choice and its importance in human behavior.

Because human behavior is not for the most part genetically specified, as it is in less complex species, man must choose if he is to act and to survive. Consequently choosing is enormously important to us. All of our moral judgments are based upon the possibility of reasonable and responsible choice. Most of our institutions — government, business, communications media, schools and universities, and so on — can be viewed as means for ensuring successful decisions in different spheres of human activity. But the deep and abiding psychic seriousness of the act of choosing is perhaps most apparent when it becomes problematic. Nothing is more abhorrent to human beings than uncertainty, and no uncertainty is more poignant and painful than that of indecision.

To choose means to decide among alternative courses of action. If there are no alternatives, there is no choice. Where alternatives exist, intelligent decision depends upon the possibility of envisaging the probable consequences of the alternatives available. When we say that a man has vision, we don't mean that he can literally see, but that he can imagine the outcome of some series of decisions — that he can envisage what the future will be, or should be, like.

Envisaging is possible only if the world is patterned in an understandable way. A random world precludes prediction. All our traditional beliefs and our empirical theories — whether in religion or philosophy, or in the arts and sciences — are constructs designed to reveal the latent order and regularity which we invariably and necessarily assume lies beneath the manifest diversity and caprice of the universe.

Understanding the world — analyzing its complex hierarchic structures, discovering its implicative and causal relationships, and discerning its subtle formal organization — is not only one of the most fundamental needs of mankind, it is also the most peculiarly human and humane activity of man. It is because such fundamental understanding is the primary function of a university that we celebrate the anniversary of Loyola.

A conception of existence — a cultural metaphysic or

ideology — is a precondition of intelligent choice. For this reason I doubt that there has ever been, or ever can be, a human society without some set of beliefs about the nature of man, the structure of nature, and the relationship between them. Because they provide a reliable foundation for prediction and choice, verified hypotheses and accurate data are obviously highly desirable. On the other hand, while a cultural metaphysic must bear a close enough relationship to reality that survival decisions are successful, it may be inconsistent, incomplete and mistaken about significant matters, yet still serve as a viable basis for behavior. Mankind has managed to muddle through aeons of error and ignorance — believing, for instance, in a flat earth, in supernatural forces controlling the universe and human destiny, in reincarnation, in astrology, and so on. Even today, our view of man and nature is fragmentary — and will probably prove wrong in many respects.

But whether or not it proves to be correct in the long run, some set of beliefs about the world is necessary if we are to choose and survive. Consider the story of the ass which starved to death while standing between two bales of hay. What it lacked was a cultural metaphysic: a reason for deciding which way to turn. This is more than a mere fable. It is a parable of the human condition in our time. But instead of two bales of hay, we find ourselves in the midst of a vast cultural supermarket stocked with a multiplicity of diverse theories and philosophies, viewpoints and attitudes, styles and slogans. And because we deprecate tradition and lack a viable vision of the future, we have no criteria for evaluating these wares — for distinguishing the genuine from the spurious, the permanent from the transient, or the significant from the trivial. As we stand thus befuddled, the purveyors of programs, fashions and philosophies blare blatant messages at us over omnipresent cultural loudspeakers urging us to select this tried tradition or that promising product, this tested style or that experimental novelty. That our age is tense, anxious and confused is scarcely surprising.

Change has been the hallmark of our time — in the arts as well as in science and technology. New styles, techniques and esthetic programs have followed one another with bewildering rapidity. Nor has the old, as a rule, been displaced by the new. Earlier movements have persisted side by side with later ones, producing a profusion of alternative styles and school, manners and means — each with its attendant viewpoint and theory.

Take the last two decades, for instance. In the visual arts, abstract expressionism and action painting were followed by pop art, hard-line painting and op art. After them came kinetic art, environmental art and a return to representation. At present all these movements coexist, singly and in combination, as alternative ways of making visual images. In music the syntax of tonality, modified in various ways, continues to be used by some composers. Some employ the serial method developed by Schönberg — perhaps extending it to the ordering of time, timbre and dynamics as well as pitch. Still other composers have used chance in composition, in performance, or in both. Often new relational principles are invented for each composition. And there have been new means: electronic music, computer music, and, more recently, mixed media works. Today all of these styles and techniques coexist, singly or in combination, as ways of composing — alongside jazz and folk music, rock and popular music. Similar diversity, though not so marked or clearly defined, can be found in literature, the theater and films. A culture which includes visual styles as diverse as those of Wyeth, Warhol and Peter Max, musical idioms as heterogeneous as those of Britten, Babbitt and the Beatles, and literatures as different as those of Bellow, Beckett and James Bond, is indeed pluralistic and perplexing.

Partly the present seems perplexing because the traditional, and still prevalent, model of history and style change is essentially linear and successive — based upon notions of evolution or progress, *Zeitgeist* or cultural homogeneity. Consequently it has generally been assumed that the rampant pluralism of our epoch is a transient anomaly, and that a single common style would eventually emerge in each, or

even in all, of the arts. This view is, in my judgement, badly
mistaken.

Contemporary culture might better be linked to what is
known in physics as a Brownian motion. This effect describes
the behavior of minute particles in a gas or liquid as they dart
about in flurries of more or less random activity. Clerk
Maxwell's image is clear and vivid. He likened Brownian
motion to "a swarm of bees, where every individual bee is
flying furiously, first in one direction and then in another,
while the swarm as a whole is either at rest or sales slowly
through the air."[3] A Brownian motion culture would be
atemporal and nonlinear. It would be pluralistic, eclectic and
inclusive. There would be no long-range cumulative developments, no goal-directed successions. No style would
"triumph" over others, and one would become obsolete.

What I envisage, then, is the persistence over a considerable
period of time, at least for several generations, of a fluctuat-
ing stasis — a variegated, but active, steady-state in which an
indefinite number of styles and idioms, techniques and move-
movements will coexist in each of the arts. Occasionally new
means and manners may be developed, but these will not
displace existing ones. The new will simply constitute addi-
tions to the already existing spectrum of styles — a spectrum
which already includes not only forms, inflections and
specific patterns drawn from earlier epochs of Western art,
music and literature, but ones taken from non-Western and
primitive cultures. Interaction among the many available
traditions may from time to time produce hybrids combina-
tions and composites; for instance, the juxtaposition of
serial techniques and materials drawn from Baroque music,
or the use of images taken from primitive art in abstract
painting. But the possibility of radical innovation seems
highly unlikely to me.

Once again history cautions us against being chronocentric.
Our is not the first period of pluralism. Competing styles and
tastes have coexisted before. What is different about our time
is not only the duration, scope and intensity of diversity, but
our bald, explicit and inescapable confrontation with it. Let
us look, albeit briefly, at how we reached this situation and,

in so doing, we will find that heterogeneity is by no means limited to the arts.

The marked pluralism which characterizes our culture began its growth in the seventeenth century. But the very ideology that nurtured diversity tended to mask its presence and obscure its significance. To believe in progress, in a dialectic of history, or in a divine plan, was to acknowledge, at least tacitly, the existence of a single force or principle to which all the seeming diversity could eventually be related. To accept a Newtonian world-view or later the theory of evolution, was almost invariably to subscribe to monism, and to look forward to a time when all phenomena would be subsumed under a single set of basic laws. The notable achievements of science led to the belief that Truth was One. Behind the manifest variety of physical, biological and social events lay, it was supposed, the latent unity of the universe which would one day be understood and embodied in a single, all-embracing model. Because there was deep faith in the essential Oneness of things, surface diversity and difference could be disregarded.

But this picture of the world is no longer convincing. The inevitability of progress, the reality of either a divine or natural purpose in nature, the existence of a single set of categorical cultural norms, and, above all, the possibility of discovering a single, ultimate truth — all these beliefs have been questioned and found wanting. Not only has no unified conceptual model of the universe been forthcoming, but diversity, both within and between fields of inquiry, has grown tremendously during the past fifty years.

In the sciences and social sciences the ideal of a single, ultimate truth proved self-defeating. The more intense the pursuit of such truth, the more fragmented the picture of the world became. In the search for first principles, new facts and phenomena kept being discovered. To study these, new disciplines were developed; to explain them, new theories were proposed. And so on. As the amount of information increased at a staggering rate, large fields became more and more divided. The social sciences, for instance, separated into anthropology, economics, geography, international studies, political science, psychology, and sociology — as well as along cultural lines: African studies, American, Asian, Balkan, Bantu studies, etc. Disciplines were further fragmented in terms of subject matter and theory. Psychology, for example, has been divided in a host of different ways: social and individual psychology, abnormal and educational psychology, Freudian and behavioral psychology, and so on.

In the arts, the sources of diversity were somewhat different, but its development was in many ways similar. During the nineteenth century an ever-increasing emphasis upon personal expression and a correlative concern for the creation of distinctively national idioms, produced marked stylistic diversity. In music, the final decade of the century held works as different in spirit and inflection as Debussy's *The Afternoon of a Faun*, Richard Strauss's *Ein Heldenleben*, and Rimsky-Korsakov's *Czar Saltan* — though all were based upon traditional tonality. During the first decade of the twentieth century, painters as disparate in manner and outlook as Cezanne, Monet and Klimt flourished. Similarly in literature, striking differences mark the work of Yeats and Kipling, Proust and Galsworthy — all of whom were active during the first years of our century. In addition, by calling attention to the value and validity of past Western art and to the arts of other civilizations, the studies of historians and ethnologists contributed considerably to the scope of diversity.

The inescapable presence of a multiplicity of styles — Western and non-Western, past and present — raised serious questions about what had been thought to be the intrinsic naturalness of particular materials and procedures in the several arts. These doubts were intensified by the invention of the twelve-tone method in music and by the development of cubism in painting. The tremendous impact of these new techniques lay not so much in their use of novel syntactic-formal means — for in many cases these were used to achieve traditional expressive goals — but in the fact that they demonstrated in a dramatic and seemingly indisputable way that *art was literally artificial.*

That works of art are man-made constructs; that traditions, far from being sacrosanct, need to be questioned and revised;

that creation consists of the impersonal invention of relational systems — all these ideas prompted a number of artists to identify themselves with and to emulate the methods and procedures of science. The work of art was no longer thought of as an expression of feelings or ideas, or as the representation of reality, but rather as the solution of an essentially artistic problem. Art, like science, was to be experimental; or like mathematics, it was to present its own self-contained set of relationships. Creativity became equated with the discovery of radical novelty, and, as a result, new idioms, movements and methods proliferated.[4]

The development of disciplines and movements has led to an inordinate increase in specialization and, correlatively, to the establishment of a large number of more or less distinct subcultures, each with its particular theories, jargon and cabal. Communication between these subcultures is tenuous at best. Advertising agents and engineers, scholars and scientists, artists and industrialists can as a rule communicate more effectively with their counterparts thousands of miles away than with their neighbors down the block or their colleagues down the hall. The situation in the sciences, described by I. Bernard Cohen, holds in varying degrees for almost every field: "Today all scientists are generally reduced to the status of laymen with respect to any branch of scientific endeavor that does not border on their own narrow specialty."[5]

Not all changes, however, have been in the direction of diversity. More efficient communication, easy travel, and economic expansion are rapidly making what were distinct and separate national and ethnic cultures more and more alike. *Time* magazine and nuclear physics, electronic music and IBM, films and modern medicine are everywhere. What is coming into being is a world culture divided into a host of separate, specialized occupational tribes.

But even if the sum total of heterogeneity has not increased, its impact has. For while ethnic diversity could be disregarded because distant cultures were considered merely exotic and perhaps backward as well, it is impossible to ignore the multiplicity prevalent *within* a culture. The options are real. They confront us directly. The pluralism of the past was no real problem. After all, one did not seriously consider adopting Chinese culture, even if one found chinoiserie charming. But a real choice must be made between advertising and anthropology, medicine and music.

In this connection, it should be noted that as specialization has increased, the possibility of moving from one field to endeavor to another has declined. And as the possibility of changing fields declines, the importance of an initial decision is magnified. Because career decisions, if not irrevocable, can be changed only with great difficulty and often entail serious penalties, choice is particularly poignant in our culture, and since it is the young who face this problem most directly, it is scarcely surprising that it is they who have reacted most desparately and drastically to the dilemma of choosing.

Finally, it its worth observing that the potential alternatives are real possibilities because our society is relatively well-off economically. The young man who, on graduation from high school, had to earn a living, had few real options. Often he had to accept any reasonable job offer. The job per se was more important than the field. But today wealth opens options, and I suspect that there is a high correlation between affluence and anomie.

Much of what seems peculiar and puzzling in contemporary culture, and particularly in the subculture of the young, can at least in part be explained as a response to the dilemma of choosing among an inordinate abundance of alternatives, and in the absence of accepted traditions and established goals. I shall begin by considering the situation in the arts, especially music, and then turn to other aspects of culture.

For the past fifty years composers have been faced with virtually unlimited possibilities and resources. Suppose that Beethoven wanted to harmonize the tone C in a piece in C major. He had only four or five alternatives to choose from, and the implications of each choice for subsequent harmonies were quite clearly defined by the syntax of the classical style. But today the same tone might be harmonized in dozens of different ways, and the implications of any one way are almost limitless in number. So too it is with rhythm, melody, timbre, loudness and so on: no generally accepted stylistic constraints limit the choices which the composer must make.[6]

Without some sort of constraints, choice is impossible. Creativity lies in the area between rigid restraint and unrestricted license. The traditional way of limiting alternatives is to accept an existing style and syntax, modifying and shaping it to suit particular needs and predilections. This way has been taken by a number of contemporary composers — Barber and Britten, Hindemith and Poulenc, Stravinsky and Shostakovich.

A second way of limiting choice has been to devise quite new constraints, ones which were systematic rather than syntactic. This was the way taken by Schönberg. For the twelve-tone method of composition is at bottom a set of rules for restricting the selection of pitches in a consistent and coherent manner. Initially only pitch was serialized. Because Schonberg and Berg accepted the esthetic of late Romanticism, its rhythmic inflections, melodic idiom and formal procedures served to limit choice in those areas. The next generation, however, found the ethos of Romanticism uncongenial. They rejected its goal-directed rhythmic, melodic and formal means. Consequently further constraints were needed, and rhythm, timbre and loudness were serialized. This was implied in Webern's music and made explicit in the works of composers such as Boulez, Babbitt, and Stockhausen.

A third and quite untraditional way of reducing the number of possible alternatives is to refuse to make particular decisions — to allow chance to choose for you. A number of composers, both here and abroad, have adopted this method of composition. But the most explicit and interesting has been John Cage. He writes:

> Those involved with the composition of experimental music find ways and means to remove themselves from the activities of the

sounds they make. Some employ chance operations, derived from
sources as ancient as the Chinese *Book of Changes*, or as modern as
the tables of random numbers used also by physicists in research. Or,
analogous to the Rorschach tests of Psychology, the interpretation
of imperfections in the paper upon which one is writing may provide
a music free from one's memory and imagination.[7]

Not only are the traditional bases for choice, such as memory
and imagination, rejected, but envisaging is specifically
repudiated. "What is the nature of an experimental action?"
asks Cage. "It is simply an action the outcome of which is
not foreseen."[8]

Artistic creation has probably always involved chance. A
melodic fragment hit upon by accident during improvisation,
or a street cry overhead during an evening stroll, have often
been turned to good purpose by composers. Similarly the
fortuitous mixing of colors on a palette, the slight flaw in a
marble block, have not infrequently influenced the final form
of the artist's work. But not until our time has chance been
elevated into a systematic principle of creation.

In Cage's music chance operations are as a rule used to
produce a fully written out score. Another way of using
chance to limit the number of decisions is to indicate, by
means of a graph or schematic drawing, only approximate
pitches, durations and so on. The realization of such a
"score" is left to the performers. They have the task of
picking particular pitches, durations, etc. Or, the composer
may fully notate a number of musical fragments each lasting
only a few seconds, leaving the ordering of these fragments
up to the performer. Finally, making particular choices may
be delegated to a computer. In this case, a set of rules are fed
into a computer which, following this program, selects
specific pitches, durations, dynamics and timbres. The end
result may be an electronic tape or a series of symbols which
can be made into a score for performance.

Similar ways of limiting choices are to be found in the
visual arts. Traditionalists, such as Wyeth and Moore, reduce
the number of decisions to be made, as did artists in the past,
by representing natural objects or scenes with varying degrees
of fidelity, and by modifying the techniques and images

inherited from some existing style. Analogous to the pre-ordering of a composition, some artists have made categorical, pre-compositional decisions which reduce the number of available possibilities — for instance, deciding to use only one or two colors, as in minimal art; basing an entire painting on a single optical illusion; wrapping objects of various kinds and sizes in paper or canvas; or building a mechanical or electronic mechanism which, once in operation, produces patterns in its own way or in response to changes in its environment. In like fashion, the use of "found" objects, whether natural or man-made, reduces the number of subsequent choices the artist must make. The object may be more or less modified, and displayed in a striking manner. But when a shoe is caste in plaster, a china doll taken apart, or an automobile motor is polished and perhaps partly painted, complex matters of form and texture, mass and color are determined with a single decision. Related to this mode of limiting decisions is borrowing visual images "found" in culture. Pop artists have done this by basing painting upon comic strips, Campbell soup cans, and photographs of Marilyn Monroe.

In the visual arts, the use of chance has been less explicit and systematic than in music. Uncalculating spontaneity, such as that involved in action painting and to some extent in abstract expressionism, however, substantially reduces the element of conscious choice and, to paraphrase John Cage, helps to provide visual images free from the artist's memory and imagination. The French painter, Georges Mathieu, for instance, is said to attack his canvasses with frenzied gestures: paint is squirted directly from the tube, or thrown, dripped and splattered on the canvas. According to Mathieu, "From now on improvisation dominates almost the whole creative act. Ideas of premeditation, reference to a model, a form, or a previously utilized device have been completely discarded."[9] If, as he asserts, "painting has rediscovered an infinite freedom where anything again becomes possible,"[10] then Mathieu is right in believing that unthinking gesture must displace conscious craft and considered choice.

In literature the problem of choice is much less pressing.

Possibilities are necessarily limited by the conventional character of a particular grammar and syntax and by the denotative nature of most words. As a result, newly invented relational systems are impractical and stylistic diversity is thereby restricted. Susan Sontag is correct in observing that there have been relatively few "experimental" novels. But she is mistaken when she implies that this is because writers are less adventurous than composers or painters.[11] It is because of the nature of language.

There have, of course, been some attempts to create an experimental literature: novels published in loose-leaf form so that the reader is required to choose among alternative plots; nonsyntactic kinds of poetry with, say, only a single word on a page; improvised theater pieces where only the outlines of a plot are suggested by the author and the dialogue is spontaneously invented by the actors, or where the actors are free to arrange their lines in various orders. A more significant sign of the need to limit choices may be the growing tendency to base new works on past ones — paraphrasing existing themes and plots, simulating established idioms and genres, or borrowing lines from particular poems or plays. For instance, Robert Lowell's *The Old Glory* is based upon works by Hawthorne and Melville, while John Barth's *The Sot-Weed Factor* simulates the style and structure of the eighteenth century novel. Music and art have used the past in similar ways. Outstanding examples would be: Stravinsky's *The Rake's Progress* based on Hogarth's engravings and employing an idiom and organization derived from eighteenth century opera; George Rochberg's *Music for the Magic Theater* which uses themes and materials borrowed from Mozart and Mahler; Picasso's paraphrases of Velasquez's painting, *Las Meninas*; and Marisol's *Mona Lisa* which is derived from Leonardo's famous work.

The proliferation of diverse styles and movements — not to mention the vast number of works available in all fields — has made choosing an increasingly difficult problem for the public as well. One indication of this has been the precipitous rise in the amount of criticism. Partly this rise is due to the growth of the academic establishment; but partly it is a response to audience needs — the need for some basis for deciding what books to read, recordings to buy, and art galleries to visit. And, with questionable success, criticism has sought to help the public understand and appreciate what it reads, listens to, and sees.

The need to limit choices is by no means the only reason for the special characteristics of contemporary music, art and literature. Cultural behavior, of which style change is a part, is the result of the action and interaction among a host of variables. Cultural beliefs and technological discovery, social-political events and scientific theories, personal idiosyncracies and intra-stylistic changes — all have had an important impact upon the arts in our time, and their influence relative to one another does not remain constant but varies from case to case and art to art. I am not, then, contending that the problem of choosing amid a myriad of possibilities is the sole causal factor shaping contemporary culture, but only that it is an urgent, compelling and pervasive one.

Turning to culture generally, even a cursory glance seems to indicate that choosing has become an important concern. Social scientists have sought to construct theories of decision-making and psychologists are studying the process of problem-solving and the nature of creativity. On a more practical level, computers are programmed, research teams appointed and consultants hired in order to help government and industry, the military and the media, decide among alternative plans and policies. Faced with similar perplexities, a number of current movements have rejected rational decision-making. Zen Buddhism, for instance, repudiates intellectual analysis and purposeful behavior in favor of direct, unmediated mysticism; Norman O. Brown urges us to repudiate ego-control and allow the Id to function freely; and existentialism espouses gratuitous, unpremeditated acts free of traditional constraints as the way to achieve self-hood. On a more vulgar level, the vogue for astrology, numerology and spiritualism, and the allure of hard, mind-blowing drugs may be seen as ways of escaping from the onerous quandary of choice.

But it is today's youth who are most forcefully affected by the prevalence of pluralism. The present generation of college students is the first to experience the full impact of diversity. Since early childhood, they have been bombarded by a continual stream of stimulation: television and film, radio and recordings, paperbacks and periodicals, and the many sounds and sights generated by technology. They have been able to taste, if not digest, philosophical viewpoints ranging from the impersonal detachment of the analytic school to the subjective involvement of mysticism, and political attitudes running from reactionary conservativism to nihilistic anarchism. The arts of all cultures — past as well as present, non-Western as well as Western, elite as well as popular — are easily available to them in paperbacks, phonograph records, and reproductions.

It is more than a matter of diversity. It is also one of sheer quantity. As fields have multiplied and education has become an important cultural concern, the amount of information and the number of conceptual constructs have grown at a stuperfying rate. The volume of scientific literature written since 1945 probably exceeds the sum total of all that was produced in the previous twenty-five centuries. The number of books and articles, compositions and art works created in a single year is awesome. The days when a single individual could cope with all areas of knowledge are gone. There is simply too much to know, and too little time in which to learn. Because only a small part of the supermarket of contemporary culture can be comprehended by any one individual, choices are continually being forced upon us.

Forced decisions are particularly painful for the young because, as noted earlier, our fragmented culture penalizes those who want to change fields. That such indecision is disturbing is shown by the fact that students who are restless, alienated, and in revolt, are frequently those who have not made career decisions. But once a choice is made and a career begun, these signs of distress and tension tend to disappear. It is not merely a matter of capitulating to the establishment. It is a matter of role- and self-definition.

Moreover, this single choice not only automatically limits the range of future options, but it defines many of the criteria for subsequent decisions.

It is not alone because they have been sated with diversity and saturated with information that a sizeable segment of college students find choosing traumatic. Having grown up and been educated in an atmosphere of permissive relativism, they tend to be skeptical — to have few firm cultural beliefs and values which would limit and guide decision-making. Even when they begin with traditional beliefs, they are often quickly disillusioned. They discover that our ideals are not matched by our behavior. As they see it, we preach the brotherhood of man, but murdered wantonly in Vietnam, we advocate democracy, while the CIA engineers military coups in South America; and we defend laissez-faire economy as people starve in the south and giant corporations pollute the air we breathe.

Dismayed by this duplicity, a number of young people have rejected ideology altogether. Traditions and goals, competition and planning are repudiated. What is valued is naive experience, unmediated by concepts and convention. The position is very similar to that of Cage and Mathieu. Calculated choice — particularly long-range planning — is depreciated. One lets the world happen as it will. What Cage says of art, these young people would apply to existence generally: namely, that it should be "an affirmation of life — not an attempt to bring order out of chaos nor to suggest improvements in creation, but simply a way of waking up to the very life we're living, which is so excellent once one gets one's mind and one's desires out of its way and lets it act of its own accord."[12] And like their counterparts in the arts, they too emphasize the importance of spontaneity, are attracted to mysticism and psychedelic experience, and want to be left to do their own thing.[13]

Reacting to the same problems, other students have adopted a very different position, analogous to that of composers and artists who devise their own rules and constraints. Though they accept no established ideology, they insist upon the necessity of choosing. They call for commitment, for a categorical decision with respect to an unequivocal, and often absolute, set of goals and values. In a sense what is sought is a kind of pre-programmed group of responses to situations, problems and persons.

Commitment is a *plus* word. Everyone emphasizes the need for it. But clearly it is not in itself a value. Commitment is for the twentieth century what "sincerity" was for the nineteenth. It may be a necessary condition for serious acts, but it is not a sufficient condition for good ones. Everything depends upon what one is committed *to*. Beethoven and Einstein were committed, but so were Napoleon and Hitler. Categorical commitment is particularly attractive in a complex pluralistic culture, because it simplifies the subtle and orders the diverse — usually into primitive polarities and convenient dichtomies.

What is involved in both these cases, as well as in career decisions, is a choice of life-styles. Such choices are important not only because they reduce the number of subsequent decisions, but because they moderate and relieve not uncommon feelings of isolation and alienation. Despite the increased efficiency of the media, interpersonal communication is often painfully precarious, particularly for those young people who have rejected established beliefs and values. For sensitive communication depends upon shared experiences and traditions, as well as upon a common language and common information. We feel comfortable with our family, ethnic group or professional colleagues because we are confident that generally speaking they will understand our behavior as we understand theirs. As society has become increasingly urbanized, it has become more complex and impersonal. Neighbors are strangers. Before a career or life-style is chosen encounters with others are difficult and uncertain. There is a sense of isolation and tension because we don't know how others will react to us. Once the choice is made, however, roles are defined, orientation takes place, and not only in-group communication but more general encounters are made easier.

Choice is, of course, inescapable. It is involved in even the simplest act — buying a loaf of bread, or turning on the TV.

In such trivial choices — white, rye or whole wheat? Laugh-in, Johnny Carson or silence? — we can be influential. What we choose, we get. But in matters of more moment, we are often much less effective. As society and its institutions have grown in size and number, they have become more complex and enigmatic, more impersonal and intractable. The inertia of established institutions reduces the effectiveness of all our decisions. Even President Kennedy supposedly despaired of really forming the State Department and the Armed Services. We are no longer confident that we are "the masters of our fate."

The young especially feel left out. In some cases they are explicitly excluded from the decision-making process. In other cases, they find it difficult to discover where and how decisions are made; and, if they do discover, it is often obvious that their influence is virtually nil. They sense that a Kafka-like network of circumstance and ill-defined responsi-bility — callous, intricate, and undecipherable — prevents them from participating in decisions and significantly con-trolling choices which will affect their lives.

It is not primarily particular individuals whom the students blame. They are also victims of the system. The fault lies in the hierarchic structure of society. *It* is the real enemy. For the young two alternatives seem possible. One (that chosen by the hippies) is to "drop out" — to refuse to become involved in the fatuous futility of social choice. The other is to try to destroy the hierarchy altogether, which is evidently the solution of the new left.[14]

In this, the final section of my paper, I should like to turn explicitly to the problem of value, particularly as it relates to the arts. I do not plan to present a set of helpful hints about how to choose and judge among works of art, though as indicated earlier this has become something of a problem. Rather I would like to consider what good the arts are, or, in current parlance, "what is the relevance of the arts?"[15]

At the outset, it is important to distinguish between "relevance *for*" some goal and "relevance *to*" some individual.

When the need for relevance is emphasized, some sort of instrumental meaning is generally involved. Sociological studies, for example, may be valued as relevant because they may help to solve the problems of the urban ghetto or the population explosion. Similarly, biology may be thought relevant because it may find a cure for cancer or improve agricultural production. The question is whether the arts have this sort of relevance.

An ancient tradition, stemming perhaps from the early association of the arts with ritual and religion, assumes that the arts are valuable because they improve morality, purify the soul, or humanize the spirit. But love of Goethe and Rilke, and devotion to Bach and Beethoven in no way prevented the personal and collective cruelty of Nazi Germany. Nor, conversely, is there any evidence that the great artists whose works are supposed to improve us were themselves specially moral or humane. But psychic unity is a myth. We all know from common experience that a devoted husband and father may be a petty tyrant at the office and dishonest in business. In view of these facts, I do not see how it is possible to maintain that men are morally improved or spiritually humanized by the works of Beethoven, Shakespeare or Michelangelo.

Some works of art have, of course, sought to influence behavior — to achieve specific goals. In this respect, however, they do not differ from essays and polemics of a more explicit sort, most of which are unread today. If the works of Dante and Goya, Aristophanes and David are esteemed today, it is not because of their instrumental value, since most of the issues are no longer pertinent, but because they continue to delight intrigue and challenge individual readers and viewers.

It seems to me that we must recognise that the arts are not primarily relevant *for* something, but are relevant *to* someone. The arts are relevant because they are entertaining. Not in the sense that the Ed Sullivan show is so — it rather diverts. But in the sense that T. S. Eliot had in mind when he said that poetry is superior amusement. For to entertain ideas — to pattern and structure the world, whether in the humanities or the sciences — and to be entertained by ideas is both the most human and the most humane condition to which man can aspire.

To some, such a viewpoint will seem hedonistic, frivolous, and perhaps even immoral. This sort of reaction derives, I think, from a tradition which begins with Plato, is continued in the Protestant view of sin and redemption, and is subsequently incorporated into social Darwinism and Marxism. In that tradition, moral rectitude is associated with hard work and sacrifice, suffering and mortification of the flesh. Artistic seriousness is confused with soulful pain or social purpose. Entertainment — the pleasure of goalless mental play — is regarded as a reprehensible, even wicked, form of self-indulgence. But the tradition of Calvin and Knox is rapidly dying, and the arts can only benefit from its demise.

But even if it is granted that the arts are primarily "relevance *to*" fields, the questions remains: to whom? Once again we must recognize the pervasive presence of pluralism. Just as there are many styles and idioms ranging from the cautiously conservative to the wildly experimental, so there are many audiences, many publics. There are, and will continue to be, audiences for popular music, folk music and art music — both Western and non-Western; for Renaissance, Classical and contemporary music; for tonal, serial and chance music; for opera, instrumental and electronic music. Some audiences will be very large, some very small. At times they will overlap, but often they will be quite distinct. A similar situation prevails, I think, in the other arts as well.

For some, this has been a cause for dismay and frustration both because egalitarian ideals suggested the desirability of cultural uniformity and because traditional beliefs about the value of art posited that an appreciation of Shakespeare or Mozart would be morally, and hence socially, beneficial. But we need not despair because only a small part of the public finds Beethoven and Mozart entertaining. For, as I have argued elsewhere, democracy does not require that everyone should like the same art, but that each person should have the opportunity to enjoy and pursue the art to which he is devoted.

Though we must allow for diversity, this does not mean that we should not educate. We teach Beethoven and Stravinsky rather than Baez, and Shakespeare and Beckett rather than James Bond, because we — our culture, past and present — have found them exciting and illuminating; and, like all lovers and enthusiasts, we want to share our delight and devotion with those for whom we care — our students. It is because we are lovers of ideas and art works that we do "our thing" and it is because we want to share that love with others that we are teachers.

Current cant calls not only for relevance, but for relevance *now*. The demand for "instant relevance" is deplorable — for it is usually both ersatz and ephemeral. To teach the music of tin-pan alley, rather than that of Haydn or Webern, because it is more immediately appealing, or to ignore Greek vase painting and *Pride and Prejudice* because they are not relevant to the Vietnam war or the problem of the ghetto is, as G. K. Chesterton put it, to sell one's soul for a pot of message.

Relevance takes time to develop and mature. It involves experience as well as formal education. Many of us have had the pleasure of rereading a book or hearing a piece of music after a period of time and feeling: Yes, now I see what it is really getting at. The question is not whether a work of art is immediately relevant, but whether it will continue to be so. To put that matter in another way: Education is not primarily a matter of intensifying existing interests and current concerns, but of developing new ones. An educated person is one to whom a broad spectrum of ideas and works of art are meaningful — that is, relevant. We must, of course, engage and interest our students. We should do so, however, not by getting them drink on the green wine of immediacy, but by teaching them, through our own ardor and devotion as well as by explicit instruction, that Beethoven is indeed more relevant — more entertaining — than Baez.

I do not mean to minimize the urgency of the great practical problems facing us. Immediate needs press in on every side. And we must deal with them soon, for time is running out. Yet we must, at the same time, realize that in the end all "relevance *for*" activities — medical research, sociology, ecology, and technological engineering — have as their goal the good life for individual men and women. Because we no longer believe in the independent existence of the state or in an historical destiny of mankind, all levels of the social-ecological hierarchy ultimately refer back to that of the individual. We must end war and the nuclear arms race, urban blight and pollution, the population explosion and disease, so that we, and those who come after us, can lead fruitful and meaningful lives.

I have not tried to propose ways of resolving the perplexities of the present, but have rather tried to understand them — to put them in perspective. This is at least a first step. The problem is partly one of learning to live with the rampant pluralism of our culture; dropping-out, categorical positions, and their esthetic counterparts are ways of coping with the problem of choice. And they will probably continue to be so. But, despite the present vogue for anti-rationalism, I suspect that there will be a tendency toward a kind of eclectic, secular humanism which will delight in diversity and dig differences. In order to comprehend a wide variety of art-styles and life-styles, there will be a concurrent move in the direction of formalism, in which the prime criteria of value will be elegance of design and ingenuity of process, precision of rhetoric and impersonality of craft, rather than emphasis upon individual self-expression or social significance.[16] The arts will be valued not because they purify the soul or promote social good, but because they involve the fun and fascination of exercising that faculty which is most peculiarly ours: namely, the human mind.

Endnotes

1. "Witches and Witchcraft," *Encounter*, 28, No. 6 (June, 1967), p. 21.
2. Quoted in *Science*, 161, No. 3838 (19 July 1968), p. 246.
3. Quoted in D'Arcy W. Thompson, *On Growth and Form* (Cambridge University Press, 1966), p. 46, footnote 2.
4. The use of science as the chief model for creativity is, I believe,

a serious mistake. Science seeks to discover new theoretical formulations. The importance attached to such discovery is shown by the fact that the scientists whose names are most familiar revolutionized our conceptions of the natural order: e.g., Galileo, Kepler, Newton, Darwin, Einstein, etc. The goal of the artist is not the formulation of general laws — indeed, he may be only dimly aware of the "rules" he follows — but the creation of a particular object or composition. The jazz musician or the Indian Sitar player, who improvises within the limits of an established tradition, shaping a specific musical experience, is creative — though he in no way revolutionizes our conception of the art of music. That such re-invention within a set of stylistic norms is of prime importance in the arts is indicated by the fact that the composers and writers acknowledged to be "great" were not for the most part those who were involved in the formation of a new style or genre, but those who built upon an existing tradition: for example, Bach, Beethoven and Brahms; Raphael, Dürer, and David; and Shakespeare, Milton and Keats.

5.   "Science and the Nonscientist," *New York Times Book Review*, April 4, 1965, p. 2.

6.   In electronic music, the number of alternatives is even more formidable. Not just twelve different pitches, but an infinite number can be produced, as can the most minute durational differences and the most intricate rhythmic complexities. Similarly, with timbre, loudness, envelope, attack, decay and all the other attributes of sound — almost unlimited subtlety and variety is possible.

7.   *Silence*, Middletown, Conn.: Wesleyan University Press, 1961, p. 10.

8.   *Ibid.*, p. 69.

9.   *From the Abstract to the Possible*, Paris: Editions du Cercle D'Art Contemporain, 1960, p. 9.

10.   *Ibid.*

11.   *Against Interpretation*, New York: Noonday Press, 1966, pp. 101f and 295.

12.   *Silence*, p. 12.

13.   My own ingrained classicism makes such facile spontaneity seem suspect, and Pope's lines come to mind: "True ease in writing comes from art not chance. As those move easiest who have learned to dance." Genuine spontaneity — that of Mozart composing the overture to *Don Giovanni* in a single night, or that of a Zen master shooting an arrow — is the result of years of disciplined training.

14.   Hierarchies are rejected not only because of the Kafka effect — the feeling that nothing significant can be accomplished within existing institutions — but also because, since they lead to fragmentation and specialization, hierarchies increase isolation and alienation.

15. It seems possible that relevance has become a problem — hence all the talk about it — precisely because in a pluralistic culture everything is potentially relevant. That is, the quest for relevance is a search for grounds for choosing.
16. These matters are considered at some length in my book, *Music, the Arts and Ideas*, Chicago: University of Chicago Press, 1967, Chapter 9.

Private and Public Art

Gyorgy Kepes

Contemporary art, in its most authentic forms, strives, above all, to bring quality and meaning into the chaotic world of our time. Those who look at it with sympathy or at least with an open mind will find that there has been a series of efforts to confront the disorder of the modern world with living values strong enough to overcome it. In retrospect, the direction of the successive stages of modern art can be distinguished quite clearly. Some stages have admittedly become ill-defined. At times the progress of modern art has temporarily slackened. There have been counter-currents, eddies, even momentary reversals, but the purifying stream of modern art has continued to flow.

When the beginnings of industrial civilization began to rob nature of its richness, when the slums of the eighteenth century were already blackening our the sun and dimming the colors of nature, Constable and Turner based their art on the need to give light, color, and space back to men hungry for the freshness of nature that seemed forever lost.

With renewed courage the serious artists of the nineteenth century sought to regain other values of our common life which were being destroyed in an age of greed. Their art developed at a time when the emphasis in human activity lay on amassing both goods and power. The immense technological advances which were made were evidently at the expense of the fuller life men had known before the industrial revolution. Mechanical progress was confusing material force with spiritual value. Things, not men, were becoming the center of the world. The new potentialities for social wealth too often led only to want and misery. Artists recognized these contradictions and sought to overcome them.

In the midst of such confusion the sense of what was honest and what was not became blurred as false ideals were allowed to mask the realities of the human condition. The painter's eye was almost alone in registering the meaningful cohesion in the world which a genuine respect for reality discloses. The "Realism" of Courbet was a conscious step toward reclaiming reality from the shams of the conventional world. Inspired by Courbet's energy and courage, other artists dared to confront the truth about the lives of men in their society. They broadened and deepened the search for truth and allowed the processes of vision itself to find expression in a more direct and natural way.

The Impressionists recognized that visual images are manmade. They realized that no representation of a visual experience, of what one believes one sees, can be a facsimile of the actual object seen; it must rather be a corresponding visual structure whose character is based upon the physiological processes by which the human eye operates. With small dots or dashes of color they broke up surfaces, rejecting the arbitrarily smooth surfaces in earlier painting. Thus, they created luminous color experiences in terms of the eye's own realities.

Cezanne went further in his attack on another kind of dishonesty. Understanding that the eye sees color in its own way, he sought to express the laws by which space is constructed by means of color. Instead of applying color to the surface of the forms in his paintings, he made color itself the central structural element of his created image. If the artist focused on certain narrow aspects of reality only, the sense of the whole was necessarily neglected and integrated form was lost. Realizing this and making others realize it also, Cezanne was a pioneer in seeking a new basic order in modern art.

Seurat, as single-minded as Cezanne, also made a frontal attack on the problem of visual order, the problem he saw as the key to all forms of creative activity and the very symbol of human aspiration. In his paintings he established structures of crystalline clarity in which all the elements worked together toward rhythm, i.e. perfection. Both artists attempted to realize that dream of order which in other ages had been the dream of religious men and which is still in one form or another the dream of all of us — the organic principle of cohesion by which every member of a structure implies and is implied by every other. The visual symbols of unity the artists provided were in sharpest contrast to the rapidly dissolving unity of the social life.

The more overwhelming the chaos and disunity of the world became, the more profound were the attempts of the artists to create images of order and the more complex the problems of expression involved. Taking their departure from the work of Cezanne and Seurat, a group of courageous younger men sought to penetrate to the basis of artistic form, clearing away the debris of the immediate past and at the same time reviving those elements of earlier art which had strength and meaning. The Cubists: Gleizes, Braque, Gris, Leger; and those who went further along the same line: Van Doesburg, Mondrian and the Constructivists, had one common purpose — to achieve strength and clarity in a new elementary rhythm of visual order in space.

Their paintings provided an architecture of color planes. This architecture compelled the beholder to follow the dynamic play of visual forces held in equilibrium. The image offered by the artist became for the observer a lively experience of order rather than a dead inventory of optical or sentimental fact. These men made no attempt to represent nature; their subject matter was order itself, apprehended as naked symbol.

Creative efforts of a more subjective character parelleled the work of those masters who sought an objective foundation for the re-orientation of art. To Van Gogh, painting was essentially an expressive human gesture and he opened his yearning heart to all things around him. Objects, he felt, were meaningful only in their human reference, and life itself, he found, was liveable only in so far as it was a common life. Embracing with passion both humanity and objects, he was consumed and finally destroyed in his desperate search for a human relationship in which man might be *for*, not *against* himself. The intensity of his search illuminated his images with the color expressive of his own searing passions.

After Van Gogh, modern art came to accept the principle that order must have an inner as well as an outer aspect, that structural lucidity in visual presentation must be matched by emotional clarity within the artists himself. The artists of our day have extended the range of modern art in the sub-jective direction by more profound explorations of the inner life and in the objective direction by more daring conceptions of visual experience. They are struggling to break out of the social stereotypes of a mechanical civilization and to main-tain their creative freedom. In doing so they are working toward a new equilibrium for the whole social body.

For, individual artistic imagination is neither self-generated nor self-contained; it belongs to the larger environmental field of nature and society. Its role and its strength con-stantly change, for the artist's responses are in a certain constant relation to the changing human conditions that generate them. The imaginative power of the artist, in its luckiest moments, creates models of sensibility and feeling that will enable all of us to live the fuller, richer life possible at this time in an everchanging world. Today, artists, like the rest of us, face a profound crisis brought about by the increasingly dynamic complexity of our social fabric. Meeting its challenge requires their fundamental reorientation in order to probe, scan, discover, absorb, change, and re-edify their surroundings. They must transform themselves as well as the social framework of the creative process. This impera-tive refers not only to the exploration of new tools and media — creating new idioms — but also to the exploration of new ways in which the work of art and the public can come together.

This necessary process, it would appear, is now taking place. Art is outgrowing its traditional limitations. The artistic forms have increased in size and acquired explosive dimensions. The isolated, sheltered, limited space of a room at home or in the galleries or museums has proven claustro-phobic for many dynamic, explosive explorations. Today, the strain is no longer limited to the physical, spatial dimension but includes the conceptual realm as well. Thus, the exhibition, the traditional medium used to create communication between the work of art and the public has had to be questioned. It has been questioned in all its implication. An exhibition, as an anthology of individual works of art and spotlighting the quality of individual work and personal achievements, no longer seems a force in the new sense of life that motivates creative expression.

Artists, even more than other men, have been displaced persons in this convulsively changing modern world. Their images, ideas, and confidence have been attuned to an older world, smaller, slower, quieter — a world they could deal with directly and endow with meaning and quality. They have not been able to deal with the new world that has burst upon them.

Artists' links with their own past, with other men, and with their environment — the very source and basis of their art — have eroded as the proliferating scientific, technical, and urban world transformed society, the physical environment that housed it, and the web of folkways, customs, thought, and feeling that gave it shape and structure.

It was hard to make contact with this apparently uncontrollable new-scale world, so big, strange, and explosive. Some artists with courage made an attempt to do so, but few could so much as establish a foothold. The extending world revealed by science exhibited unfamiliar vistas of phenomena and concepts: things too big to be seen, too small, too hidden; ideas too evasive to grasp — subnuclear particles, the indeterminacy principle, computers and transistors, lasers, pulsars, DNA, and inorganic crystals that could change into organic viruses and back again. Few of these were accessible to the ordinary human sense or were capable of being related to the human bodies that men use to find their bearings.

The wildly proliferating man-made environment rapidly shrank living space, polluted air and water, dimmed light, bleached color, and relentlessly expanded mass, dirt, noise, speed, and complexity. The changing society exploded with problems on an immense scale: ecological disasters, social tragedies, eroded individuality, confused and impoverished human relationships. The expanding vulgar realm of mass communications and commercial entertainment deadened sensibilities and was as inane in meaning as it was sophisticated in technology and aggressive in its destruction of privacy and leisure. Life and art were separated from each other; and both seemed torn loose from their common social foundations.

Aldous Huxley's comment that by mistreating nature we are eliminating half of the basis of English poetry is an understatement. The world around us — the luminous, mobile wonders of the sky, the infinite wealth of colors and shapes of animals and flowers — is the core of all our languages and is basic to our sensing of quality and meaning in life.

We have contaminated our rivers and killed Lake Erie by dumping detergents and excrement. We poison our sky, sea and land with radioactive waste. By overexploiting and exhausting our land we have created menacing ugly erosions. We shave barren our mountains, hills, and fields — exterminating birds, fish, and beasts. This fearful destruction of the rich surface of our environment goes far beyond extermination of what some consider lower forms of nature. It is symbolic of our situation that in the 1968 meetings of the United Nations the subject discussed with the deepest concern was the devastation produced in our precious earth, sea, and air, by reckless manipulation of technological power.

Some artists were like distant early warning systems of the human condition today. They read the signs of coming ecological and social disasters early and with full grasp. They saw the illusion and the degradation at the height of compacency in the last century over what was believed to be the best of all possible worlds. Their confident understanding of the sensed qualities of living structure would not permit them to accept the nineteenth century mechanical models of scientific analysis as an adequate framework for breadth, freedom, and self-variation of life and art. We were not unwarned about the lethal consequences of the wholesale devastation of the natural landscape. With the first blows of industrialization in the opening years of the nineteenth century and the appearance of belching chimneys and mountains of slag, the poet Blake cried out against the "dark Satanic mills" that had defiled "England's mountains green" and "pleasant pastures." He was joined by fellow artists and poets in a chorus of angry protest; but light in the industrial landscape continued to gray with soot and rivers to turn brown with sewage. William Morris summed it up over a century ago. "It is only a very few men who have begun to think about a remedy for it in its widest range, even in its narrower aspect, in the defacements of our big towns by all that commerce brings with it, who heeds it? Who tries to control their squalor and hideousness? . . . Cut down the pleasant trees among the houses, pull down ancient and venerable buildings for the money that a few square yards of London dirt will fetch; blacken rivers, hide the sun and poison the air with smoke and worse, and it's nobody's business to see to it or mend it: that is all that modern commerce, the counting-house forgetful of the workshop, will do for us herein.

. . . Yet there are matters which I should have thought easy for her; say for example teaching Manchester how to consume its own smoke, or Leeds how to get rid of its superfluous black dye without turning it into the river, which would be as much worth her attention as the production of the heaviest of heavy black silks, or the biggest of useless guns." ("The Collected Works of William Morris," Volume XXII, pp. 24-25. New York: Russell & Russell, 1966. Delivered before the Trades' Guild of Learning, December 4, 1877.)

Yet only now, at what may well be the very last moment, have we begun to turn our minds toward solutions. There are more tragic and more hurtful aspects still. Who with clear eyes and honest mind can deny the urgency of resolution of the inhuman blight of our contemporary cities? Some of us hardly dare to walk with our heads up, knowing and seeing how men mistreat men. Many of us are tortured by our impotence to act to counteract the destruction of what is best in man. The aborting of the quality and sometimes the very basis of lives because of narrowness, prejudice, and vested interests is the shame of all of us. Though people in increasing numbers recognize the urgency of finding means to redirect our collective suicidal life, for the time being we are carried along by the momentum of our situation: we continue to develop ever more powerful tools and equipment without having the sense of values that tell us how to use them.

The explosiveness of this time compels us to question all the basic assumptions of the previous generation. Current history calls upon us to adjust ourselves to change faster than men have ever needed to in the past. Each new phase of development, each new bit of knowledge, each new technological power has intensified the continuing struggle between the old inherited guiding concepts, feelings and attitudes and the new requirements of reality. Dickens began his tale of the French Revolution with the following sentence, "It was the best of times; it was the worst of times." This comment fits no time better than our own. Every age, no doubt, has an option between a good and a bad life. Every age has a spectrum that ranges from suffering to fulfillment, but none has presented these options with so sharp a contrast as our own. Like the men of every age, we have alternative potential futures. But today these alternative futures range from a concrete promise of richness, quality, and security of life that men could never have dreamed of before to the menace of a destruction that could wipe out everything mankind has accumulated, everything that it values.

We seek equilibrium, the optimum condition possible in our circumstance. Individually and collectively men are self-regulating systems. In order to achieve our goals we must learn to proportion our efforts or flow of efforts to the flow of return information. In order to achieve these goals we need an understanding of the reality of the goals, and must allow our sensors or abilities to scan life's circumstances and to gather the data required by our recognized tasks. An engineer who designs a self-regulating system must learn to synchronize error and correction of error in order to avoid "hunting" — excessive oscillation about his target point caused by inaccuracy of aim. Every purposive movement is composed of two processes, not one; their symmetry in action is the measure of the success of the process. Central to a self-regulating system is the notion of feedback, or, to express it more generally, interdependence. We have not found, in our exploded explosive age, the right method of self-regulation. The good life, the maximum realization of the intensity, quality and gross potential of individual lives to which all of us aspire, is achieved when we find a balance with minimum hunting — a minimum of human suffering and wasted energy with a maximum of helpful relevance for all of us. For this we need an acute awareness of interdependence. In other words, we need a social standard based upon full cooperation between man and man, and between man and nature. We have not found this yet, and the wild oscillation of our social and cultural life is the reflection of an unresolved historical stage.

The most eloquent display of our frantic search for a resolution may be found in the antics of twentieth century artists. The vehement, erratic, continuous transformation of artistic idioms, the changing morphological dimension, the continuous shifting of the rules of the game in expressive artistic form-making are charactersistic of the contemporary life of the arts. What is most significant is that the artist's search is not only characterized by the repeated redefinition of artistic idioms but also involves basic changes in the artist's frame of reference, his existential stance, and his basic assumption concerning the meaning, the role, and the purpose of art. After thirty or forty years of soul-searching concerning the language of art, the artists of today are questioning more than the means by which to express themselves. They are questioning the very meaning, the very foundation of their activities. Today there are not only movements of art *isms*, there are also a basic confrontation between art and antiart or no art, the most critical self-confrontation of the validity of making art or not making art.

But the forces that are rending art and society are not less than the forces that are bringing them together. Artists are key men in a reorientation that seems to be taking place; they seem to be regaining their long lost role of cultural leadership. Paradoxically, the displaced persons of yesterday are beginning to look like Moses figures who will lead us into a Promised Land. After a long period of "hunting," their homeostatic processes of automatic regulation have shifted to relationships in which they are beginning to regulate; the artists will indeed find solutions to their problems provided they base their rich responses firmly on an uncompromising sense of life as a whole — a passionate solidarity with humanity and with the natural and man-made environment.

Contemporary life, in a very direct way, is making us aware that it is possible to meet the new levels of scale and to undertake the restructuring of our existence. The new relationships being formed between the individual and his social and physical environment have made it clear that the time has passed for viewing man as an isolated creature who can be examined separately from his place and responsibilities. We feel the need for the reestablishment of dissolved and broken links, for a union of man and his surroundings, for concrete expression of the new relationships. The quest for it is taking place everywhere, and large numbers of men in a variety of fields are searching for the key to new knowledge. What is more, as they turn to one another for opinions and answers, they are beginning to sense it.

During the past two decades some of the freer and more speculative minds among scientists have focused fresh attention upon the old idea that biological and social evolution are closely linked, with intercommunication playing the same role in social evolution that interbreeding once played in biological evolution.

Today we are in a critical stage of the human phase of evolution. Evolution is becoming self-conscious, and we have begun to understand that through social communication it is within our intellectual and emotional power to come to better grips with our existential reality. Our future, good or bad, depends upon how clearly we understand and how well we control the self-regulating dynamic pattern of our common existence as it moves into the future.

To coordinate our efforts it is necessary to agree on objectives. To agree on objectives it is necessary to reach a better common understanding of "reality."

What we are calling reality here is neither absolute nor final. Rather, it is itself an evolutionary pattern continually generated by the evolutionary process, as Charles Sanders Peirce had recognized some seventy years ago. "What anything really is, is what it may finally come to be known to be in the ideal state of complete information, so that reality depends upon the ultimate decision of the community; so thought is what it is only by virtue of its addressing a future thought, which is in its value a thought identical with it though more developed. In this way, the existence of thought now depends on what is to be hereafter; so that it only has potential existence, dependent on the future thought of the community."

Awareness of the dynamics of evolutionary continuity and our capacity for self-transformation by inter-thinking has opened up rich wide new perspectives. Our potent new tools, both conceptual and physical, contain within themselves an important aspect of these perspectives. For the more powerful devices we develop through our scientific technology, the more we are interconnected, interacting, interwoven with each other, with our machines, with our environment, and with our own inner capacities. Each new tool of vision that science and technology prepares for us opens up a new landscape that compels us to see in its interconnectedness that the farther we can travel and the faster we move, the more we see, understand, and learn about other parts of the world and other people's lives. The more sensitive and embracing our feelers of vision, hearing and thinking become through radio, television, and computer technology, the more we are compelled to sense the interaction of man and his environment. Our new tools of transportation, communication, and control have brought a new scale of opportunities to inter-thinking and inter-seeing; the condition of a truly embracing participatory democracy.

The advancement of creative life — and, likewise, of human knowledge — is produced by the interaction of the whole community. All society has become an intricately interacting system that can survive only through the intricately inter-connected workings of its members. Through the communication of the knowledge and insights of creative men in many fields, we have the opportunity to make all that is valuable within us a shared possession — a new "common" property of all who seek a higher quality of life.

The "common" realm, as we may name our shared body of thought and feeling, is a generator of human creative powers. The vital artists of this moment of time are converging upon this realm. They are guided by a growing new sense of the structural principle of interdependence. They are beginning to accept interdependence personally, professionally, and ecologically — which is to say, in the balance that modern man so urgently needs to establish with the total of his environment. The artists' current work — it is not too much to assert in consequence — exhibits growing optimism, strength, and authenticity. It looks toward a future art scaled to the expanding scientific-industrial urban world and revealing its latent richness.

Artists are finding in our environmental landscape a new material of plastic art, a potent source of creative objectives. They dream of molding gigantic artistic structures carved from the earth, resting on the ground, flying in the sky, floating in the ocean, that are themselves environments.

Cutting through suffocating cultural isolation, many of them have crossed disciplinary lines and joined hands with scientists and engineers. This collaboration has made available to them the creative tools for imposing technical sophistication: computers, lasers, complex electronic devices, and also the tools for tasks of gigantic dimensions, i.e. the large-scale handling of power. A centuries-old discarded framework for the artistic process, thus, has been revived in the newest evolutionary step in the development of the artistic community. In becoming a collaborative enterprise in which artists, scientists, urban planners, and engineers are interdependent, art clearly enters a new phase of orientation in which its prime goal is the revitalization of the entire human environment — a greatly-to-be-wished-for climax to the rebuilding of our present urban world.

The artist, just as clearly, in addressing himself to such a task, forges a new relationship of social responsibility with

respect to his fellow man and a new relationship of interdependence between man and his environment. The tasks
that he takes on are different from previous tasks in kind as
well as in scale. The values that he uncovers become the
values of the rest of us, giving sharpness and definition to our
sensed need for union with our surroundings and intimate
involvement with them. This emerging creative world is
illuminated by the interplay of social needs, increasing knowledge of tools and techniques, the relevant in philosophic and
artistic heritage, the full sweep of the physical and social
environment, individual imagination, collective vision, and a
wide spectrum of contemporary scientific knowledge. This
developing embracing vision of the artists, we may hope, is
prophetic of a new world outlook pervaded by a sense of
continuity with the natural environment and oneness with
our social world. This oneness is something we long for, a lost
paradise of the human spirit. All of us, at rare and lucky
moments, have had the feeling that everything fits together
and makes sense, that the world is right and full of promise.

Contemporary anthropology, psychology, and applied
science all bring us converging messages that the evolutionary
key to the resolution of major disturbances in our individual
and common lives rests in achieving a harmoniously functioning human ecology, a state in which we recapture on the high
level of today's advanced cultures something of the union of
man and his surroundings achieved by earlier and more primitive cultures. We know that the new unity to be sought
between man and man, and between man and his environment
and to which we may hopefully look forward will need to be
fundamentally different from that of the Taoists, preclassical
Greeks, and Hopi Indians. It may well be, however, that
through correct reading of our current situation we can make
effective and realistic use of our scientific competence to
project the creative insights that will midwife a new human
consciousness and weld the converging fragments of a
possible future into a satisfying and enduring reality. That
reality can take on the aspect of an "ecological climax," a
dwelling for the human spirit not unlike the dimly remembered Garden of Eden from which advancing knowledge

now beckons us to return.

Anthropologists, in studying early cultures, have re-awakened our sense of ecological harmony. Early man, like a modern primitive, saw himself as an inseparable part of his group or society and his society as an indivisible aspect of all-embracing cosmic surroundings. Natural phenomena existed only as directly perceivable human experiences that were nevertheless aspects of natural cycles or cosmic events. There was a oneness of man and men, of men and their surroundings. Each sign coming from the outside had meaning in human terms; and each human act was considered to be an inevitable and irreversible consequence of the happenings or events in the surrounding natural world. In this interwovenness, there was no consciously discerned subject-object confrontation. For us the subject-object separation is paramount; without it no scientific knowledge would be possible. It became central to our thinking when the ancient Hebrews demoted the sun, moon, and forces of nature to mere ornaments of a transcendent God who had made everything and was above everything.

The outside world appears to us in a hierarchy of organizations, beginning with the higher animals and descending through plants to inanimate, physical, chemical, atomic, and subnuclear processes. For the primitive man there was no break in the spectrum of life. Life was everywhere, in men, beasts, plants, stones, and water. For the Australian Bushman, the pearly iridescence of sea shells, the sparkling of a crystal, the phosphorescent glow of the sea at night, and the sunlight caught in droplets above a waterfall are all signs of an embracing, living thing, the basic link seen as the great snake whose body arches across the sky in the rainbow. Everything is permeated by life. Everything seems in contact, interacting, interliving. In the simpler stages of human existence, on the level of children and the primitive world, the connection with the environment is almost as intimate as the unity of the body itself.

The experimental evidence of modern psychology gives further support to this view. Our reactions to the environment are not those of independently functioning discrete systems but of a total organism. Whenever outside forces impinge upon our sensors, a relative equilibrium tends to be established through the mobilization of our entire self, regardless of what sense organ is immediately involved in receiving and registering the impacts from the outside. There are no separate sense modalities; all levels of sensory function are interdependent and blend together. They are furthermore in a fundamental union with motor processes. A dynamic perception theory in which sensory processes are apart from motor functions is not even conceivable in modern psychology.

Applied science, too, provides us with thought models of dynamic interconnectedness and basic complementarity of disparate processes and systems, particularly in such fields as computer technology, electronics, and communication networks. Such technologies seem almost to plead to be integrated with life, to clarify ecological disorder, and to play an important role in realizing ecological climax. For this is the realm of the new-scale tools by means of which the making of things is automated, astronauts rendezvous precisely in the vast ocean of space, facsimile pictures are sent over telephones, sound becomes light and light sound, and the cycles of nature are reversed, the darkness of night becoming another day. The capacity of this realm to guide us, mold us, and transform us is beyond calculation. We are given a model of interdependence on a cosmic scale.

A report published by the National Academy of Sciences in 1967 hints at the awesome symmetry of the promises and menaces inherent in our potent technology. Contracts were awarded to some aerospace companies for studies of the feasibility of oribiting a huge satellite to reflect light from the sun onto the dark side of the earth. Among the possible uses listed for such a solar mirror were to provide artificial lighting levels greater than full moonlight for nighttime illumination of search and rescue operations, recovery operations, security areas, and polar latitudes. Critical reaction came immediately from astronomers concerned that the lighting of any large area of the night sky to a brightness several times that of full moonlight could jeopardize observational astronomy. Other scientists pointed to the possible harmful effects on the daily and yearly rhythms of plant and animal life.

The complementarity of technological and social awareness can be fused into unity if we face squarely our present urgent social needs to combat ecological disasters, further develop consciousness of social interdependence, and build the sense of living freely according to ways in which everything fits together.

The artists are in a strategic position to bring all these issues together in a living focus. There are signs that they are ready to take on this important role. First, they have reached out to make effective use of the new-scale tools. Second, they are ready to participate in new-scale tasks, to take leave of the small, suffocating spaces of rooms and exhibition galleries and to participate in a bigger environment on a bigger scale than ever before. Third, they begin to open their eyes to the present ecological tragedies. A sensibility that subsumes a highly developed ecological consciousness will find the way to expression of ecological tragedy, just as the sensibility of a previous day could engage itself with great human tragedies. In one and the same form, the tragedy of the environment can be dramatized and means can be provided to recycle unsightly waste and convert a scene of ecological regulation into a stirring focus of civic art. The sense of beauty and the sense of purpose — the patrimony of the artists — can be conveyed to others who do not quite understand these things but who do understand almost everything else. The great-scale tasks to be performed with the new tools need urgently to incorporate the deepest qualities of human consciousness. This cannot be done without artists.

No doubt, we are approaching an epic age in which the emphasis will be placed on major common obligations. There is a need for those who have the imaginative power to discern the essential common denominators of this complex late twentieth century life. There is a need for those whose loyalty is undivided, who can devote their abilities to the epic tasks. But whatever emphasis we wish to and must put on our common goals, in the final reckoning both the beginning and the end of action lie in individual experience. As individuals, all of us live on many levels and experience diverse life qualities. We work, we play, we cry and laugh, we sleep and dream, we fear and hate, we make love, and on rare occasions, we feel the single climactic glow that comes when the distilled essences of our experiences are amalgamated into a unified understanding. This process can occur only within the individual. But great things would emerge if the optimum of individual experience — the artist's poetic insights — would become an integral part of our common life. Only the realization of a dynamic complementarity of the personal and civic can offer the possibility of living up to our immense potentialities.

PART V

PHILOSOPHY AND VALUES

Social Values and Technological Change

A Case Study: Social Welfare and Personal Happiness

Nicholas Rescher

Philosophers are notoriously reluctant to grapple with the empirical details of transient circumstances. It is their aspiration to deal with timeless truths seen *sub speci aeternitatis*. But alas, this ideal is unrealizable in the area of human values. Values are a *social* reality. Unlike the timeless physical realities that concern the *natural* philosopher — the permanent features of physical nature — the *social* philosopher confronts a sphere of kaleidescopic change. Values, in particular, must be seen in a social context, and this social context changes. It is thus most appropriate that the present symposium be held under the rubric of the *Current Evolution of Man's Sense of Value.* And these considerations also account for the fact that in much of what I say I shall sound, perhaps, as much like a social psychologist as like a philosopher.

To illuminate the stresses and strains that current socio-economic tendencies create for our sense of values, I propose to consider two particular values that are especially near and dear to the core of current idealogical thought: *social welfare* and *personal happiness*. My interest in these specific values is, however, motivated by a more general — and so perhaps more philosophical — objective. For the tensions and difficulties that will be seen to arise here illustrate and indeed typify the generic impact of social and technological change upon our value system as a whole.

It seems like a self-evident truism to maintain that the aim

163

of measures for promoting the welfare of the people, to "improve their lot," is to make them happier. One speaks of the *social welfare* of a group with a view primarily to the extent to which its members enjoy certain of the generally acknowledged requisites of happiness, including health (physical and mental), material prosperity, education, protection against the common hazards of life, and the like. The link seems almost tautological: even as an increase in his monetary standing improves a man's condition in point of wealth so — it might appear on first thought — must an increase in his welfare standing improve his condition in point of happiness. But unfortunately, the matter is not actually as simple and straightforward as all this. The linkage of welfare to happiness is not only more subtle and complex, but — worst of all — more remote. We shall, in fact, shortly see that these are factors that can obtrude themselves between welfare and happiness and can intervene so as to render improvements in the former (welfare) nugatory as far as improvements in the latter (happiness) are concerned.

For present purposes, "happiness" should be understood as the sort of *perceived happiness* that is at issue when a person asks himself: "Am I really happy these days?" This involves a mixture of (primarily) two considerations: (1) an assessment of mood-patterns, ie, some sort of averaging of the state of his psychic feeling-tone of euphoria/dysphoria over the recent past and the predictable future, and (2) an intellectualized appraisal of the conditions and circumstances of his present mode of life with a view to his content or discontent therewith. Both these ingredients — the mood-aspect and the satisfaction-aspect — are essential components of happiness. The man who, from the angle of intellectual appraisal, finds no basis for discontent (he enjoys spendid health, affluent circumstances, has good family relationships, etc.) may possibly still fail to *feel* happy; the man who sees himself as deeply unhappy may yet continue in a euphoric state of "feeling happy" (perhaps even through drink or drugs).

The substantial improvement that has occured in the general standard of American life throughout the period after

World War II — with which we shall be concerned here — is readily documented. As regards health, the life-expectancy statistics tell a seemingly straightforward story: In the course of the single generation from 1940 to 1970, the expectation of life of Americans, at birth, has steadily increased from just under 63 years to just over 70 years. In the decade from 1958 to 1968, the average American added a full year to his expected healthy lifespan (i.e., time free of expected bed-disability or institutionalization).

There has also been a steady improvement in the financial status of Americans. In the period from 1950 to 1965 the personal income *per capita* thus saw an increase in real income of some 29 per cent.

It is also a significant fact that Americans are increasingly better educated. Between 1950 and 1965 the percentages of the population, between 5 and 34 years of age, enrolled in school increased substantially (44 to 60 per cent), and the percentage of adults enrolled in educational programs more than doubled. This quantitative increase, moreover, fails to reflect the qualitative solidification in American education in the post-Sputnik era.

There has also been a truly dramatic growth since World War II in America's public investment in social welfare measures. The social welfare expenditures *per capita* under public programs, measured in constant (1958) dollars increased fourfold between 1945 and 1965, doubling in the first five postwar years, and doubling again since then. Moreover, not only have circumstances improved with respect to the necessities and basics of life, but with regard to the luxuries as well: Just in the decade from 1955 to 1965 *per capita* consumption expenditures for recreation thus increased by 26%, and in the same period, *per capita* consumption of tobacco grew at a modest pace, while *per capita* expenditures for grooming and care came close to doubling.

Taken together, these statistics bring into focus the steady and significant improvement in the circumstances of individual well-being and social welfare that has taken place in the United States since World War II. If the thesis that increased welfare brings increasing happiness were correct, one would certainly expect Americans to be substantially happier today than ever before. *This expectation is not realized.* Indeed, the available evidence all points the reverse way.

A substantial body of questionnaire data have been completed over the recent years that make possible a survey of trends in the self-evaluated happiness of Americans. Operating with increasing sophistication, various polling organizations have made their rounds making massive samples of representative Americans to appraise themselves in point of being "very happy" or "fairly happy" or "not happy" — or the usual "don't know." (See Table 1) No doubt there is a

Table 1

Selfclassification of Americans in Point of Happiness
(Results of Some Questionnaire Studies)

Year (Organization)	% Very Happy	% Fairly Happy	% Not Happy	% Don't Know	"Score"
1946 (AIPO)[a]	39	50	9	2	110
1947 — [a]	38	57	4	1	125
1949 — [a]	43	44	12	1	106
1957 (SRC)[b]	35	54	11		102
1963 (NORC)[c]	32	51	16		83
1965 (NORC)[c]	30	53	17		79

a. Data from Hazel Erskine: "The Polls: Some Thoughts about Life and People," *Public Opinion Quarterly*, 28, No. 3 (Fall, 1964).
b. Data from Gerald Gurin, Joseph Veroff, and Sheila Field: *Americans View Their Mental Health*. Basic Books: New York, 1960, p. 22.
c. Data from Norman M. Bradburn: *The Structure of Psychological Well-Being.* Chicago, 1969, chap. 3, table 3.1. See also Norman M. Bradburn and associates at NORC: *Reports on Happiness.* Chicago, 1965.
Note: In computing the "score" we set *very happy* = +2, *fairly happy* = +1, *not happy* = −2, and *don't know* = 0.
AIPO = American Institute of Public Opinion, Princeton, New Jersey (Gallup Organization).
SRC = Survey Research Center, University of Michigan.
NORC = National Opinion Research Center, University of Chicago.

certain looseness in these data collected by somewhat different procedures by different organizations.[1] But a relatively clear and meaningful picture emerges all the same: Around a fairly stable middle group of "fairly happy" people (some $50 \pm 5\%$ of the respondents) there is, during the 1941-1965 period an erosion of the sizable initial very happy group, resulting in a near doubling of the category of those who class themselves as "not happy." A relatively clear trend emerges: With the passage of years since World War II Americans on balance perceive themselves to be increasingly less happy.

The evidence just considered relates to the *subjective* impression of the people interviewed. But there are also relevant data of a more objective kind that indicate a failure of Americans to achieve a higher plateau of personal happiness in the wake of substantial progress in the area of social welfare.

The suicide rate per 100,000 population per annum has hovered with remarkable steadiness in the 10.5-11.5 region ever since World War II. Moreover since 1945 a steadily increasing number of Americans are being admitted to mental hospitals, and, on the average, are spending an increasingly long stay there. Such overt indicators reenforce the available evidence based on personal impressions to suggest that it would be the very reverse of the truth to claim that the impressive post-war progress in matters of human welfare has been matched by a corresponding advance in human happiness. How is this striking fact to be accounted for?

The sought-for account can, it would seem, be given in something like the following terms: an individual's assessment of his happiness is a matter of his personal and idiosyncratic perception of the extent to which the conditions and circumstances of his life meet his needs and aspirations. And here we enter the area of "felt sufficiency" and "felt insufficiency." A person may quite meaningfully say: "I realize fully well that, by prevailing standards, I have no good reason to be happy and satisfied with my existing circumstances, but all the same I am perfectly happy and quite contented." Or, on the other hand, he may conceivably say, "I know fully well that I have every reason for being happy, but all the same I am extremely discontented and dissatisfied."

In this context we get back to the old Epicurean proportion:[2]

$$\text{degree of satisfaction} = \frac{\text{attainment}}{\text{expectation}}$$

The man who personal vision of happiness calls for yachts and polo ponies will be malcontent in circumstances many of us would regard as idyllic. He who asks but little may be blissful in humble circumstances. It is all a matter of how high one aspires in point of expectations.

On this basis, it becomes possible to provide a readily intelligible account for the — on first view startling — phenomenon of increasing discontent in the present era of improving personal prosperity and increasing public care for private welfare. For what we are facing is an *escalation of expectations*, a raising of the levels of aspiration in the demands people make upon the circumstances and conditions of their lives. With respect to the requisites of happiness, we are in the midst of a "revolution of rising expectations" a revolution that affects not only the man at the bottom, but operates throughout, to the very "top of the heap."

This supposition of an escalation of expectations regarding the requisites of happiness finds striking confirmation in the fact that despite the impressive evidence that people think of themselves as less happy than their predecessors of a generation or so ago, they would be quite unwilling to contemplate a return to "the good old days." Let us examine this evidence.

Over the past thirty years, various polling organizations have again and again asked Americans questions like:

Do you think Americans are happier and more contented today than they were 30 years ago?

Modern Technology has made many changes in the way in which

people live today compared with 50 years ago. On the whole, do you
think people are happier now because of these changes than they
were then or not as happy?

Uniformly, the result on such questionnaires has been to
maintain time and again — usually by a ratio of 2 to 1 or
more — that Americans were happier in the earlier period.
Recognizing the improvement in the circumstances of life as
regards health, knowledge, the bulk of representative
America respondents perceive themselves as living in days
when there is less peace of mind, more to worry about, and
correspondingly a decline in the general level of personal
happiness.

In the face of such a widespread consensus that Americans
were happier a generation or so ago, it would seemingly
follow that people would hanker after "the good old days."
We might expect to find that many or most people would
prefer to have lived in this bygone, happier time. So, indeed,
it might well appear. But the actual fact is just the reverse
of this expectation: I will cite just one example, a Roper/
Minnesota poll of 1956.

If you had the choice, would you have preferred to live in the "good old days" or the present period? (Roper/Minnesota, 1956)	*Yes*	*No*	*Other*
	15%	57%	29%

These findings are quite typical. Invariably Americans reject
the would-have-lived-then-rather-than-now option by a ratio
of better than 2 to 1. What are we to make of this? I think
the answer is clear. So emphatic an indication of the un-
willingness of people to trade their circumstances for those
of what they have themselves judged to be a happier time,
suggests that Americans have come *to expect more* of life
if a given level of happiness is to be realized. Their view seems
to be: "To be sure, given what little people asked of life
in those 'simpler' days, what they had was quite sufficient
to render *them* happy, or at any rate happier than we are
today — we who have more than they. But, of course we,
with our expectations, would not be very happy in their
shoes." This position makes sharply manifest the phenomenon

we have spoken of as an escalation of expectations.

As our Epicurean proportion shows, when increased expectations outstrip the actual attainments — even significantly growing attainments — the result is a net decrease in satisfaction. An important lesson lurks in this finding, viz, that the idiosyncratic happiness of its members is of itself a poor measure of the attainments of a society in the area of social welfare. It would only be a good measure in a society whose expectations held fairly constant, or, if not that, at least developed in a "realistic" manner, ie, in a gradualistic pattern that did not automatically leap beyond increasing attainments.

We have noted the impressive signs of improvements in the social welfare status of Americans in the years since World War II. But these welfare gains have — to all appearances — been rendered fruitless for the corresponding augmentation in personal happiness that — seemingly — was "only to be expected." It would appear that the hard-won victory was spoiled by an escalation of expectations that countervailed against the actual realization of the satisfactions to be gained, transforming the summer of our glories into the winter of our discontents.

This, then, is a summary of the past situation. But what lies ahead? In contemplating the future much is uncertain, but one thing is sure: so long as the escalation of expectations continues, there is a bitter ultimate price to be paid in the hard coin of disillusionment. To continually "raise one's sight's" with regard to the requisites of happiness is to become more and more of a utopian, to come closer to insisting upon the *millenium NOW*. But this, of course, is just not in the cards.

It would seem to be a plausible supposition that in the first approximation, people's expectations of future improvement in the general circumstances of life (or a future deterioration, for that matter) are largely based upon an intuitive *extrapolation of the current trends and tendencies*. But notice now what must happen if we are concerned with a course of improvements occuring at a decelerating rate — as we always eventually must be whenever the phenomenon

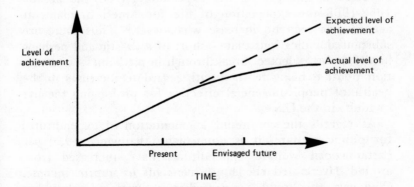

with which we are concerned improves in an asymptotic (and so ultimately limited) manner — than disappointment is pretty well inevitable. For in all such cases when we face what an economist might call a temporal course of diminishing marginal returns, the simply extrapolated *expected* future levels of achievement must inevitably fall short of the level *actually* attained in the future.

Just this situation seems to obtain with regard to many aspects of social welfare. We are nearing the end of the line on improvements in certain significant areas of public welfare. Most of the welfare improvements we considered at the outset are subject to a kind of saturation.

First, with regard to the prospects of continuing improvements in the general health, let us take a closer look at American life expectancy statistics. We have seen that in the two decades between 1945 and 1965 the expectation of life at birth increased by more than four years, from just under 66 to just over 70 years. But this seemingly dramatic increase is deceptive, being largely the result of two factors, a decrease in infant mortality and an improvement in the health standards of nonwhite Americans. Thus when one looks at the corresponding figures for white adult males one finds that the increase over these two decades is slightly more than half a year, from 69.5 to 70.1 years. Indeed, since around 1955, the previous increase in life expectancy has leveled off for

American males, despite any contrary impressions based on increases in the general life expectancy. Over the decade 1958-1968 the expectation of life for American males at age 65 has seen no increase whatsoever.[3] Thus there are substantial indications that — short of a drastic and perhaps hardly to be expected, breakthrough in medicine — a saturation point is being reached with regard to increases in the health of people-in-general effective for prolonging the life of adults in the U.S.

As regards the continuing augmentation of expenditures for public welfare, it is noteworthy that since 1950 *per capita* social welfare expenditures have increased from around 10 to around 15 per cent of *per capita* income. Obviously this trend has neared its saturation level. It has been estimated reliably that in 1964 Americans committed $31 billion — some 5% of the Gross National Product — to federal anti-poverty programs alone.[4] These figures indicate that — regardless of what the actual *need* may be — the (real) social welfare expenditures cannot be expected to be raised significantly beyond present levels. (Politics, after all, remains "the art of the possible.")

Moreover, we are managing to make no improvements at all in our attempts to reduce certain major causes of unhappiness in the form of the malign vicissitudes and traumas of life, such as crime, accidents, and the collapse of family relationships. I need not dwell at length on the fact that growth in crime rates is a matter causing widespread alarm. In the short period from 1960 to 1965 the rate of crime of violence against persons increased by almost 25%, and property crimes by over 35%. The rate of motor vehicle thefts increased by 40%. In 1968 alone, over 800,000 cars were stolen in the U.S., an increase of 23 per cent over the previous year which itself saw an increase of 17 per cent over its predecessor.[5] In the latter 1960s one in seven Americans feel victim to a reportable crime. (In cities, of course, one's chances are worse still).

And corresponding to this increase on the side of the perpetration of crimes, there is a corresponding increase in the magnitude of loss on the side of its victims: Between

1950 and 1967 the property loss in theft per $1,000 of appropriable property grew from $2.12 to $3.91. Thus the overall risk of theft per $1,000 of property has come close to doubling in this 17 year period.

Again, injuries and deaths by accidents — and especially automobile accidents — show no signs of any significant abatement. In 1969, 20 million Americans were injured by pesticides, flammable fabrics, electric appliances and other common but hazardous products used in and around the house, and some 18,000 died of such injuries.[6] All in all, the rate of death by accidents in the U.S. per 100,000 population has held remarkably steady at around 6 per 10,000 population throughout the post-war period, and there is little chance that this can be brought down as long as automobile accidents fatalities continue their disconcertingly healthy growth-rate (from 21.5 in 1950 to 26.5 in 1965 per 100,00 population).

Nor does the extent to which people suffer nonfatal illnesses and disabilities seem to be subsiding in any significant measure. Thus hospital admissions per 1,000 population per annum have increased from 110 in 1950 to 145 in 1965.

And not only are people more likely to go to the hospital than before, they also tend to *stay* there for longer periods. On the medical side, life-prolongation does not tell the whole story as regards happiness. Illness nowadays may be less significant as a cause of death, but no less prominent as a source of annoyance, misery, debility, and frustration. The very nourishment in which we seek sustenance is a potential source of danger to us: it has been estimated that in 1969 over 2 million Americans became ill from eating con-taminated food.[7] Although Americans *live* longer than in former years, they do not seem to be all that much healthier on a day-to-day basis.

The family has always constituted one of the main pur-ported sources of personal happiness. But here again the statistics underwrite no cheering inferences. The incidence of divorce, for example, has been a remarkably stable pheno-menon throughout the post-war period. Moreover, the much-publicized increases in juvenile crimes and delinquency

offer yet another indication of a failure to realize higher
levels of family happiness.

The precise interpretation of all such statistics can, of
course, be argued with here and there. Statistical evidence,
in general, invites argument. (The increased crime rates may
to some extent merely reflect better reportage; the increased
hospitalization rates may to some extent be the result of
more extensive resort to hospitalization insurance of various
types, and so on.) But the over-all picture is clear enough.
Despite substantial progress with regard to the social welfare,
little progress — and perhaps even some retrogress — is being
made in bringing about a reduction in the traumas and
tragedies of everyday life. Prominent among the principal
factors in human happiness are such items as (1) physical
health, (2) mental health, (3) prosperity, (4) personal security in ways other than financial, and (5) family life. The
available data show an unqualified improvement with regard
to only one of these, namely, prosperity. As regards one
other — physical health — we may very well be nearing the
"end of the line" as far as continuing general improvements
are concerned. And with respect to the rest, there is little
ground for speaking of improvement in the sources of personal happiness, since the facts point in a reverse direction.
The statistical data we have canvassed thus incline to support
rather than conflict with the previously given impressionistic
indications of a decrease in the general level of happiness
among Americans.

However better off he may be in certain limited (albeit
unquestionably important) respects, the individual faces a
pattern of life in contemporary society in which the grounds
for unhappiness and anxiety are still — as ever — impressively
prominent. We are all familiar with other, perhaps less readily
quantified aspects of this phenomenon: the intense and in
many ways threatening pace of technological and social
change; the depersonalization of life under conditions of
urban crowding and congestion; man's pollution and destruction of his natural environment; the ever more strident blare
of the media of "communication"; the anxieties of life in
the shadow of the atomic sword; the quickening pace of

alcoholism and drug dependency; the ever shifting yet ever present manifestations of social and economic discrimination and deprivation; the decline in the moral climate and the increase in pornography, venereal disease, and illegitimacy. Substantial improvement in significant sectors of the conditions of life not withstanding, the potential sources of unhappiness, while here and there removed or diminished, show, or balance, little or no tendency towards abatement.

Something akin to a *principle of the conservation of negativity* is often operative in human affairs. Anyone who has decorated their own home or cared for their own garden knows that once the worst eyesore has been removed, the next-to-worse can leap into a place just about equally prominent and dissatisfaction-creating. It is a "fact of life" that the achievement of real progess need not be accompanied by any commensurate satisfactions. And there is nothing perverse about this: it is all very "natural." Man tends to be a creature of discontents — be they divine or otherwise. The imminent goal once achieved, simply "raises his level of expectation" and presses onwards to the next goal.

One result of this tendency is what might be characterized as the phenomenon of *hedonic discounting*. This is best explained by an analogy. It is a familiar commonplace that the stock market primarily responds not to the present economic facts, but to anticipations of the future. Making present allowance for foreseeable future economic improvements (or declines) the market has already *discounted* them by anticipation when they become a reality, and so under-reacts to or even ignores major achievements when they occur. A parallel phenomenon seems to occur in the context of foreseeable improvements in the conditions of human life; a similar under-valuation of realized achievements in the light of prior expectations. Having expected as much (or generally more) we simply refuse to recognize very real achievements at their own true worth. When progress is realized it is discounted as regards its real contribution to happiness: by the time an achievement is made, we have already "raised our sights" in anticipation of its successors.

But if the escalation of expectations in regard to the

requisites of happiness — whose nature and scope we have
here endeavored to elucidate — continues, then a tragic time
of reckoning lies ahead. The considerations we have canvassed
point to the ironic conclusion that advances in welfare
have in the past — through their promotion of an escalation
of expectations — been self-defeating from the standpoint
of happiness: they have brought in their wake a diminution rather than an increase in "the general happiness" of
Americans.

Different times bring different situations. Franklin D.
Roosevelt's dictum that "We have nothing to fear but fear
itself" may have been apposite in the America of the
Depression. But now circumstances are otherwise, and to a
significant extent it is today optimism that constitutes a
threat, and not pessimism. Danger lurks in an unrealistic
confidence in utopian progess that expects that the circumstances of life should every day in every way be getting
better and better. There are good grounds for thinking that
unless the "revolution of rising expectations" in matters of
human welfare is sharply curtailed, a period of increasing
disappointment, discontent, and disaffection lies in wait.

This era of disillusionment is no remote and distantly
prophetic prospect, but a developing reality whose initial
stages can already be discerned in its early stages in the
domain of current fact. A significant — if not yet substantial
— sector of the most privileged, intelligent, and socially
aware among American youth are turning their back upon a
society that has not provided their generation with the
millenium. Accepting the facile hedonism and the escalation
of expectation that is rife in the society about them, they
contrast the idyllic picture painted by such exaggerated
expectations with the harsher realities of the actual facts. The
result is a kind of social schizophrenia, an inability to accept
and come to grips with the actual environment, marked by
the usual schizoid symptom of withdrawal ("opting out") and
the corresponding tendency towards irrationalism. Insistent
upon achieving *now* more than is possible — given the state of
society and of technology as they actually exist — the trend
is not merely to impatience, but to defeatism regarding man's

ability to solve man's problems.

The result is to turn one's back not only upon modern science, but upon rationality itself — to indulge oneself not merely in antiscientism but in unreason as well. A substantial number of young Americans are even now traveling down this road in a "flight from reality" into the sphere of drugs and black magic. From the reality of instant coffee and instant shaving they have sprinted on to the fiction of instant happiness (and instant knowledge and wisdom as well). Here is the bitter fruit that grows in the garden of the *millenium* — that ultimate product of what is not just an escalation but a run-away *inflation* of expectations that must — if the social order is to remain viable — be brought, somehow, under control.

Currently there seems to be an open season on the communications media — it is a time when they are subject to blame and reproach from many quarters. Yet it seems not unreasonable to hold them to task in our present context. In dwelling on the marvels of science, in their insistence that the difficulties of the moment can — if only we want it badly enough — yield to a happy resolution in the near future, and in depicting the twenty first century as the dawning of a new and wondrous world, a time when all the present shortcomings of life will somehow be transcended, the media contribute powerfully to that millenial tendency of thought that — in my view — presents one of the gravest dangers of our time.

This brings me near to the conclusion of my discussion. I have tried to carry through in detail a case study of the relationship between two key values of modern western social ideology, viz, social welfare and personal happiness. I hope I have succeeded in persuading that the linkage of welfare to happiness is more subtle and complex — and unfortunately far more remote — than it seems at first view.

The considerations canvassed in this paper have important implications from the standpoint of social welfare. The promotion of welfare is concerned not with providing for the happiness of people as such, but with increasing the accessibility of certain generally acknowledged *requisites* of happiness, so as to bring about improvements in the "climate of life." Thus — as we have seen — a potential gap remains open between the public welfare and personal happiness. The prospect remains that in a society in which many or most achieve what people-in-general regard as the basic requisites of happiness may yet by and large fail to be happy. From the present standpoint, it is entirely possible (if seemingly unlikely) that one could improve the quality of life of people without in fact making them any happier — a prospect particularly acute when people are "unrealistic" in their demands upon life. The juxtaposition of the two topics of my paper — viz, *social values* and *technological progress* — thus has its ironic aspect. For its appears that we may well be deprived of the advantages of the latter by malign developments in the former sphere, with the fruits of the cornucopia of technology eaten away by the worm of unrealism in our values.

Endnotes

1. For example, the Gallup people used "fairly happy" for the middle group while NORC and SRC used "pretty happy."

2. One of the few empirical case studies I am acquainted with that revolves about this bit of speculative philosophy regarding the relationship between expectation and (probable) achievement is: Arnold Thomsen: "Expectation In Relation to Achievement and Happiness," *Journal of Abnormal Social Psychology*, 38 (1943), pp. 58-73.

3. U.S. Department of Health, Education, and Welfare, *Toward A Social Report*. Washington, 1969, p. 3.

4. *The War on Poverty: A Handbook*, National Catholic Coordinating Committee on Economic Opportunity (September 29, 1964), p. 24.

5. Data from M. J. Wilson: "Auto Thefts Being Stripped of Amateurs." (Newsweek New Service Study), *The Pittsburgh Press*, Nov. 28, 1969, p. 21.

6. Data from Richard D. Lyons: "Trouble Over Drugs on the Market," *New York Times*, Jan. 4, 1970, "News of the Week in Review" section 1, p. 5.

7. Richard D. Lyons: *op. cit.*

The Contemporary Criticism of the Idea of Value and the Prospects for Humanism

Emmanuel Levinas

Humanism can be defined as a conception of the world which asserts the existence of an irreducible human essence, clothed with a value or a dignity which makes it the aimed at end of being. This definition, a very ambitious one, would suit Biblical humanism. In this latter is to be seen the bond which attached humanism to the idea of value and the difference which distinguishes the ideas of value and being — a difference, moreover, which in placing the idea of the Good over and above essence goes back to a venerable philosophical tradition.

But humanism can be understood in a less radical way, a way less certain of ultimate finalities which regulate the universe — a less metaphysical way in the pre-Kantian sense of the term. The humanism of the Renaissance wanted to hold itself to an immanent teleology of the human. All eschatology would deny man the absolute mastery of his own destiny and, consequently, would alienate him. But Culture is substituted for the supernatural. In it, humanity is its own end, its own value — a finality which is vouched for in the identity of the Self with himself prior to all acts of identification and without reference to anything *else*, a finality which is thus vouched for in the freedom of the Self, an identity prior to all acts of identification and indispensable for these acts, an identity of the *I think*, of the Reason, a finality of one's self, visible first of all in self-consciousness,

179

in the interiority of the free and rational Self. Man is value, and as such he stands out from the order of Being or nature.

But the claims of humanism can be limited even more. The progress of the natural sciences which humanism glorified ends up with the discovery of the conditions for the human in nature. It compromises its autonomy. Certainly, transcendental philosophy subordinates nature and the whole of being to human reason, to the unity of apperception, to the identity of the I think. But the man who thus asserts himself is a man who is logically constructed. All that which his inner experience brings him, all that which he finds as an objective value in culture is subordinated to the sieve of universality. His passions, his particular drives are considered as merely psychological or subjective. These are pejorative words. Only the universal forms of civilization are saved from this depreciation. The depreciation strikes also all cultures other than occidental. Such is the status of value and man in the Kantian perspective.

Humanism and axiology have another meaning in the second half of the nineteenth century and the first half of the twentieth. The neo-Kantians attached to Lotze, Windelband and Rickert on the one hand, the phenomenologists such as Max Scheler on the other, thinkers such as Lask and Nicolai Hartmann who join together the two influences — the neo-Kantian and the phenomenological — Rene Lesenne and Louis Lavelle in France — all develop a notion of value and valuing free from subjective arbitrariness, a trans-subjective notion of valuing and value, but a trans-subjectivity distinct from the order of being and in this in agreement with the Platonic teaching of the good which is over and above essence, a trans-subjectivity — and this is the new feature — which is inseparable from the concrete interiority of man, from the free and personal self where values are *verified* and *realized*. It is no longer the formal characteristic of universality which imposes value on an impersonal reason and transforms it into a person; on the contrary, it is man — man as an emotional fullness and also an intentional affectivity who is indispensable for the manifestation of value. Value thus is seen to have a material content. A value determined in its content, irreducible to logical structures and experienced by man in his valuing — such is the new idea. Referred to the test of experience, distinct from the experience of the given, value is not being.

Value is not added onto a reality like a quality; it situates *given* going in a dimension which is not that wherein determination and indetermination are distinguished. In their being-of-value beings have a different status from that which corresponds to their being-perceived. It is completely *otherwise, different*, completely separated from the *really* or the *truely*. But the *meaning* of this *otherwise* is inseparable from human freedom, and the contact with valuing flows back on man and raises him to the status of value. The notion of value exalts and consecrates the notion of man. Humanism thus preserves a strong meaning.

Less ambitiously defined than in the Bible or in the Rennaissance, it means, on the one hand, that the human cannot be reduced to the nonhuman and, on the other, that — and here one will notice its phenomenological origin — all intelligible meaning, be it logical or mathematical, refers back to human meanings. Human meaning, this certainly does not refer to the rational animal, a part of nature; rather it is always a relation between a desire and a value in an ambiguity. One can say equally well that desire confers value or that value elicits desire.

Such a conception of value and humanism is exposed to very serious criticisms in our time. Is the distinction between being and being-of-value sufficently drawn so as to lead us beyond being? Language which suffices for all utterances and which one treats today as an almighty God is in a position to tie together by means of the copula all value as an attribute to a subject and to thus reduce valuing to a quality — an operation which refers back to the understanding of being, to the understanding of an objectivity which is the natural ground of attribution. The *beyond* and the *completely other than being* of valuing is, as a result, understood as modalities of being, as *adverbs* relating to the verb *to be* — as if ontology, the understanding of the being of beings, exhausted all the problems.

As a result, the human is no longer eccentric in regard to being, no longer extra-ordinary; it is put back into its place, and the verification of valuing of which it seemed to be the crucible leads no farther than any other experience whatsoever. Henceforth, the baseness of the ideological — in the Marxist sense of the term — is tied to all that is human but which is not to be found in the orbit of knowledge or in a rational politics. Being would be without an exit, and man would be certainly one of the high places where the designs of being work themselves out, but a high place where these designs work themselves out without man's knowledge. This certainly does not necessarily imply the un-freedom of man. Human freedom can even be called for by the manifestation and the articulation of structures. In this sense, the whole activity of the scientist and of the political is found to be in the service of being, values intervening in this activity only to rise with men and to draw them all the better into the service of being.

Values and humanism are thus called into question in our time by reason of the development of the human sciences. But Heidegger, the most contemporary philosopher — a philosopher formed by phenomenology itself which is so important for the notion of value — confirms this calling into question.

The human sciences distrust the inner man in the interest of scientific rigor. The self who listens to himself and feels himself out, defenseless against the illusions of his class and the delusions of his possible neurosis is denied by psychologists, sociologists, historians and linguists. A formalistic methodology which is less confident in axioms than it is interested in axiomatics seeks to master the wild proliferatin of human facts by emptying them of their content.

This is methodological anti-humanism which, psychoanalytic, Marxist, structuralist, fights for science against ideology, scorning values petrified in the form of *belles lettres*, without a hold on the real, violent and unhuman. Indeed, is it admissible that the authenticity of values revealed by the so-called human interiority as beyond being may be thought to be unreal like a product of ignorance, narrowness and laziness? But this crisis in humanism, this distrust of interiority stems from an even deeper deception of our times.

The action encompassed by technology which should have brought comfort, liberal politics which prevents neither exploitation nor war, a physics which is called upon to encompass the world and which turns it over to disintegration — this apocalyptic inversion of human projects could be attributed to social alienation and leave open the hope of a recovery. But our century has known revolutions which have degenerated into bureaucracy and the violence of crimes rigged out in revolutionary appearances. The very work of dealienation becomes alienated as if the adequation of the self with himself were impossible, as if interiority where formerly values were experienced could not close itself in on itself, as if the self in his presence to himself failed to coincide with himself and missed himself. For these identities the human sciences substitute mathematical idealities outwardly identifiable. Everything is outward. This is perhaps the strongest definition of materialism and, in any event, the end of interiority — of this state within a state, of this world within the world, of one of those sub-worlds off of which metaphysics has lived.

The end of metaphysics, the end of humanism — this is the thesis of Heidegger. Man as a subject identical with himself, certain of himself in the cogito, capable of closing himself in on himself, and thus interior man, man who in his psychological life experiences values in himself and who in his cultural life extends a meaning to nature, the man of humanism, in the beginning a stranger to that nature which he enlivens — this man would be the creation of European metaphysics which is on the verge of ending.

To this metaphysical notion of the interior man, Heidegger opposes a man whose existence is but the manifestation of the *esse* itself of being. Human existence is meaning and word. It is not the exteriorization of any interiority whatsoever but the reply to the silent language, to the opening which opens up this very *esse* of being. Human speaking is but a speaking from the depths of a hearing. Being is directly and first of all opening, site, hospitality, place, world. The strangeness of the world for man which the subject would have to render livable by incorporating into it values experienced in his interiority would be but the aberration of a metaphysics and a humanism which is nearing its end.

I ask if the strangeness of man in the world is not perhaps but the effect of a spiritual process begun with the Presocratics who taught the opening of being without however their teaching having prevented the forgetting of the opening in and through Plato, Aristotle and Descartes? I ask if the crisis of interiority is the end of this strangeness. Does the crisis of the values of the so-called inner life call into question the primordial value of the human? Such are the questions which must be clarified in concluding.

The notion of a man exterior to being and exiled on earth is older than Greek metaphysics and has certainly already directed the development and orientation of this metaphysics towards the idea of a man foreign to the world. Do not we Westerners, from California to the Urals, nourished on the Bible at least as much as on the Presocratics, do we not feel a strangeness in the world which owes nothing to the certitude of the Cartesian cogito and which the end of metaphysics does not succeed in overcoming? Have not the Sacred Scriptures read and commented on in the East given a new slant to the Greek writings? I am not inclined to believe that they have simply been written in the form of a palimpsest in regard to the latter.

In Psalm 119 we read: "I am a stranger on earth, do not conceal your commandments from me." According to Biblical criticism, would this text be late and would it go back already to the Hellenistic period where the Platonic myth of the soul exiled in the body could have captivated the spirituality of the Orient? But the psalm alludes to texts which are recognized as being prior even to the century of Socrates and Plato, notably in Chapter 25, verse 13 of Leviticus: "No land shall be irrevocably alienated, for the earth is mine, for you are but strangers dwelling in my abode." It is not a question here of the strangeness of the eternal soul exiled in the world of fleeting shadows, of a separation from home in inhospitable regions which the erection of a dwelling and the possession of land would allow to be overcome in releasing, by means of the erection of a dwelling, the hospitality which this site envelops. For in Psalm 119, in the context of this *difference* which is proclaimed between the self and the world, are to be found the commandments, those which impose an obligation towards other people.

An echo of the Bible's permanent mesage and perhaps its principal message, this condition — or un-condition of — stranger and "slave in the land of Egypt" draws man together with his neighbor. Men seek themselves out in their uncondition of strangers. This latter unites humanity. The difference which accounts for this strangeness in the world is fundamentally a nonindifference in regard to men — in regard to value.

Free man is chained to his neighbor; no one can save himself without other people. The guarded preserve of the soul does not close in on itself from the inside. It is "the Eternal which closed the door of the Arc on Noah," a text of Genesis tells us with a wonderful precision. How could it have closed itself at the time when humanity was perishing? I ask if there is ever a time when the deluge does not threaten. Here is the impossible human interiority claimed by the anti-humanism of our times. It derives neither from metaphysics nor from the end of metaphysics. There always being a distance between the I and the self, the recurrence of the I to the Self is impossible. It is impossible, for no one can remain in himself, for the humanity of man is a responsibility for all. The return to the self turns into an endless detour. Before being consciousness, choice and agreement, the humanity of man is human brotherhood. It is responsibility which constitutes Man and which is the source of values. This is not the responsibility which a constituted subject, existing in himself and for himself like a free identity, assumes but rather that of the man of unlimited responsibility, unlimited because not measured by my engagements, responsibility for the others toward whom the movement of recurrence, in the very entrails of the subjectivity which it tears apart, is found to be turned.

Stranger to himself, obsessed by others, uneasy, the Self is a hostage, a hostage in his very recurrence to himself, never ceasing to fail to measure up to himself, but always in this way ever closer to others, ever more indebted, aggravating his own self-bankruptcy. This debt does not get reabsorbed except by getting larger.

Having no rest in one's self, without any bias in the world, this strangeness to every place, this being-on-the-other-side of being, this beyond — this is certainly an interiority in its own way. It is not a philosopher's construction but the unreal reality of men persecuted in the concrete history of the world of which metaphysics has never grasped the dignity and the meaning and from which the philosophers turn aside their heads. Responsibility in humility, a humility which is not only the most basic of virtues but a condition of man beneath consciousness where humanisms and axiologies have their origin, since conscious humility is already pride.

This responsibility undergone beneath all passivity, from which one one can free the Self unable to close in on himself, responsibility from which the Self cannot escape, a self for whom the Other cannot substitute himself — this responsibility points thus to the unicity of the irreplacable Self, an unicity without interiority, a Self without rest in himself, a hostage of all others, turned away from himself in every movement of his return to himself, a man without identity, this is to say, a constant prey to the crisis of humanism but precisely thereby called upon to be a man.

Modern antihumanism is no doubt right when in man conceived of as an individual in a genus or a being situated in an ontological region, persevering in being like all other substances, it does not discover a privilege which would make of him the aimed at end of reality or when it calls into question man as a being belonging to no genus, to no ontological region but only to his interiority.

But it is also necessary to think in starting from a responsibility always older than the conatus of the substance of interior identity, in starting from a responsibility which always calling one outside of himself upsets precisely this

this interiority, in starting from one's self, a hostage of all, substituted for all by his very un-interchangability, a hostage of all the others who, precisely as others, do not belong to the same genus as myself since I am responsible for them without having to worry about their responsibility in my regard, for even for that I am in the last analysis and above all responsible. I ask if in this way the Other Person is not a value. Modern anti-humanism is perhaps not right in not finding in man, lost in history and the order of things the trace of this responsibility which makes a subjectivity and, in the other person, the trace of this value.

A Note on Contributors

KENNETH E. BOULDING Professor of Economics and Program Director of General and Social Dynamics, University of Colorado. Graduate study at Oxford, University of Chicago. Recipient of sundry honors and fellowships. Author of *Economic Analyses*; *Economics of Peace*; *The Organizational Revolution*; *The Image*; *The Skills of the Economist*; *Disarmament and the Economy*; *The Meaning of the Twentieth Century*; *Beyond Economics: Essays on Society, Religion, and Ethics.*

WM. THEODORE DE BARY Horace Walpole Carpentier Professor of Oriental Studies, Columbia University. Graduate study at Columbia, Harvard, Yenching and Lingan universities. Awarded numerous fellowships. Author, co-author or editor of *The Buddhist Tradition*; *Self and Society in Ming Thought*; *Approaches to Asian Civilization*; *A Guide to Oriental Classics*; *Problems in Asian Civilization*; *Sources of Japanese Tradition*; *Sources of Indian Tradition*; *Sources of Chinese Tradition.*

MIRCEA ELIADE Sewell L. Avery distinguished service Professor, and, Chairman of the Department of the History of Religion, the University of Chicago. Graduate study at Bucharest and Calcutta. Recipient of many honors, awards and fellowships. Author of *Yoga: Immortality and Freedom*; *Shamanism: Archaic Techniques of Ecstasy*; *Images and Symbols*; *The Myth of the Eternal Return*; *The Forge and the Crucible*; *Patterns in Comparative Religion*; *Myth and Reality*; *Myths, Dreams and Mysteries*; *The Two and the One*; *From Primitives to Zen.*

189

VIKTOR E. FRANKL Professor of Psychiatry and Neurology, the University of Vienna; Head of the Department of Neurology at the Poliklinik Hospital in Vienna. Guest lectureships at sundry universities; world lecture tours. Author of *Artzliche Seelsorge*; *Psychotherapie in der Praxis*; *Der umbewusste Gott*; *Der unbedingte Mensch*; *Homo patiens*; *Theorie und Therapie der Neurosen*; *Man's Search for Meaning*; *Psycho-therapy and Existentialism*; *The Doctor and the Soul*; *The Will to Meaning: Foundations and Applications of Logotherapy*.

ROGER GARAUDY Professor in the Arts Faculty, the University of Poitiers. Graduate study at the Academy of Sciences, U.S.S.R. Author of *Les sources Francaises du socialisme scientifique*; *La theorie materialiste de la connaissance*; *La liberte*; *Humanisme marxiste*; *Perspectives de l'homme*; *From Anathema to Dialogue: A Marxist Challenge to the Christian Churches*; *Le grand tournant du socialisme*; *Christian-Communist Dialogue*.

GYORGY KEPES Professor of Visual Design, and Director of the Center for Advanced Visual Studies, the Massachusetts Institute of Technology. Creative work in painting and graphic design. One-man and group exhibitions of paintings, and recipient of a number of prizes, awards and fellowships. Author, or, editor of *The Language of Vision*; *The New Landscape in Art and Science*; *The Education of Vision*; *Structure in Art and in Science*; *The Nature and Art of Motion*; *Module, Proportion, Symmetry*; *Rhythm: Sign, Image, Symbol*; *The Man-Made Object*.

EMMANUEL LEVINAS Professor of Philosophy, the University of Paris at Nanterre. Graduate study at the universities of Charkov, Kaunas, Strassbourg, and the Sorbonne. Additional study with Edmund Husserl and Martin Heidegger. Author of *La theorie de l'intuition dans la phenomenologie de Husserl*;

De l'existence a l'existant; *En Decouvrant l'existence avec Husserl et Heidegger*; *Totalite et infini*; *Difficile liberte*; editor of Edmund Husserl's *Meditations Cartesiennes*.

ROBERT K. MERTON Giddings Professor of Sociology, Associate Director of the Bureau of Applied Research, Columbia University. Graduate Study at Temple and Harvard universities. Holder of sundry distinguished lectureships and fellowships, and recipient of various awards and honors. Author of *Science, Technology and Society in Seventeenth Century England*; *Mass Persuasion*; *Social Theory and Social Structure*; *Studies in the Scope and Method of the American Soldier*; *Social Policy and Social Research in Housing*; *The Focussed Interview*; *On the Shoulders of Giants*; *On Theoretical Sociology*.

LEONARD B. MEYER Professor of Music, Chairman of the Department of Music, the University of Chicago. Graduate study at Columbia and Chicago; studied musical composition with Stephen Wolpe, Otto Luening, and Aaron Copland. Author of *Emotion and Meaning in Music*; *The Rhythmic Structure of Music*; *Music, the Arts, and Ideas*.

NICHOLAS RESCHER Research Professor of Philosophy, Associate Director of the Center for Philosophy of Science, the University of Pittsburgh. Graduate study at Princeton. Recipient of various awards and fellowships. Editor of *American Philosophical Quarterly*. Author of *Hypothetical Reasoning*; *The Logic of Commands*; *Many-Valued Logic*; *Topics in Philosophical Logic*; *The Development of Arabic Logic*; *Temporal Modalities in Arabic Logic*; *Studies in Arabic Philosophy*; *Essays in Philosophical Analysis*; *Values and the Future*; *Introduction to Value Theory*; *Distributive Justice*; *The Impact of Technological Change on American Values*.

RODERIC NINIAN SMART Professor of Religious Studies, Chairman of the Department of Religious Studies, the University of Lancaster. Graduate study at Oxford with John L. Austin, and at Ceylon in Eastern religions. Holder of various lectureships and fellowships. Author of *Reasons and Faiths*; *A Dialogue of Religions*; *Historical Selections in the Philosophy of Religion*; *Philosophers and Religious Truth*; *Doctrine and Argument in Indian Philosophy*; *The Teacher and Christian Belief*; *The Religious Experience of Mankind*.

Index

196   *Index*

Swami Vivekananda   19, 21

Technology, and values   23,
 61, 92-105, 148, 157, 174,
 178, 183
Teilhard de Chardin, Pierre
 43, 45
Third world   98
Thompson, D'Arcy, law of   39
Theory of value   31
Totalitarianism   72
Transformation ratio   31, 32
Trevor-Roper, H.R.   117-18
Tribal society, and white
 frontier   24-5

Value(s),
 and art   117-41, *passim*;
 135 ff
 and artists   135, 146, 151,
 158
 and community   153 ff
 and economics   31, 32-46
 and efficiency   95
 and humanism   179-87,
 passim
 and labor   95, 102
 and Marxism   95-102,
 passim
 and Social Welfare   163-78,
 passim
 and will to meaning   71-91,
 passim

Value(s)—*cont.*
 as relevance to, or, for   136,
 146
 attitudinal   86
 creative   86,95
 economic   31-46, *passim*
 experiential   86
 internal preferences   40
 Marxist   95-102
 of city   7-8
 of house   9-10, 11
 of world   4-16, *passim*
 religious   6 ff
 social   163-77, *passim*
 trichotomy of   86 ff
 world   5, 6
  of form and value   4
Van Gogh, Vincent 145-6
Vietnam   45, 133

Weber, Max   52, 58
Welfare economics   38,
 163-78, *passim*
 system   44
White frontier   2, 3, 19
Will to meaning   71-91,
 passim
 to pleasure   77
 to power   77

Youth,
 and decision-making   135
 and pluralism   132 ff
 and responsibility   83 ff